EMPIRE BUILDER

THE ROAD TO A BILLION

EMPIRE BUILDER

ADAM E. COFFEY

Cheval Press

EMPIRE BUILDER
The Road to a Billion
First Edition

ISBN   979-8-9890491-2-7 *Hardcover*
         979-8-9890491-1-0 *Paperback*
         979-8-9890491-0-3 *Ebook*
         979-8-9890491-3-4 *Audiobook*

This book is dedicated to JT Foxx, whose vision kickstarted this project, and to the countless entrepreneurs who attended Mega Success in Anaheim and the inaugural Empire Builder event in Dallas. Little did you know that your presence at these gatherings paved the way for the creation of this book. With unwavering determination, you traveled from all corners of the globe, seeking knowledge and tools to build and refine your own empires.

I also extend this dedication to the multitude of individuals who support me tirelessly on social media, devour my books, attend my speaking engagements at universities, and contribute to the diverse enterprises I've built.

Lastly, this dedication is for all those who dare to dream of achieving that elusive billion-dollar exit. May this book serve as a beacon of inspiration and guidance along your ambitious path.

CONTENTS

A QUICK NOTE ON PROFESSIONAL ADVISORS

Building an empire is a complex journey. Along the way, there will be many instances where the need for specific, fact-based assistance will be required. These legal, financial, tax, accounting, and other personal or business-related issues will require you to employ the expertise of duly licensed professionals who are fully conversant with the details of your life, your business, and the many intricacies of local, state, and federal law.

This book is not intended to provide financial or legal advice, steer you in a particular direction, or answer any specific questions that you might have. This book is also not a substitute for getting the necessary, specific, and fact-based advice from the professionals described above. Rather, it is intended to serve as an aid to help stimulate your own creativity while building an empire. My hope is that it will give you more confidence and clarity for the road ahead.

Empire Builder is not a work of fiction. It is based on recollections and reflections from my personal experience across several decades. I have done my best to recount certain specific events that have shaped my thinking on building an empire; however, I am human, and I reserve the right to have made a few mistakes along the way. Truthfully, I wish I had been given all of my books forty-one years ago when I was graduating high school and heading off to boot camp in the United States Army. My journey to build an empire would have been much easier and even more fruitful.

That said, thank you, dear reader, for walking this path with me. Check the box on my legal disclaimer. Now, let's get on with the work of building *your* empire!

LAYING THE FOUNDATION

Over the past thirty-five years, I've met and worked with thousands of entrepreneurs from all around the world. There is one thing they all have in common: they are dreamers. They dream of being their own boss, changing the world, growing their wealth, and—perhaps most of all—building an empire.

These aren't just idle daydreams, either. They are powerful drivers, spurring millions of people to take action and start their own businesses. As of 2022, in fact, over 33 million small businesses existed in the United States. That's more than 99.9 percent of the businesses in this country!

Unfortunately, there's a big problem: once they've started their businesses, many entrepreneurs don't know how to take the next step and turn their dreams into a sustainable reality—and the data reflects this. According to the Bureau of Labor Statistics, 18 percent of small businesses (defined in the US as less than 500 employees) fail within their first year. That means, of the 5,044,748 new businesses that were started in 2022, almost 1 million will close their doors in 2023.

Even if a business survives its first year, it's by no means out of the woods. Fifty percent of small businesses fail within five years, and approximately 65 percent don't make it more than ten years in business.

These statistics are sobering and, frankly, scary. But, they're also why I wrote this book. During my thirty-five-year entrepreneurial journey and billions of dollars in exits, I have learned the formula that can consistently take businesses in any industry from startup to a billion dollars or more. In short, I've learned the secrets to building empires. And now, I'm going to share those secrets with you.

WE CAN BEAT THE ODDS AND BUILD AN EMPIRE

If you've read either of my first two books (*The Private Equity Playbook* and *The Exit Strategy Playbook*), you already know some things about me and my career. (And if you have, thank you, constant reader, for joining me again—and welcome back!) But if you are starting with me for the first time, you may be wondering what gives me the right to claim

I can help you not just beat the odds, but build a true empire.

It's a good question—one I think is best answered by sharing a bit about my background.

Each of us has key moments in our lives that shape us into who we are. My first key moment came right out of high school when I joined the US Army. Serving in the military was pivotal for my development. It taught me leadership, discipline, and teamwork. It was, in fact, the foundation for my becoming what we now call a "servant leader." The army honed my moral character and taught me how to lead—both by example and from the front.

The education and experience I got in the service were the foundation for my life as a CEO, an entrepreneur, a best-selling author, a coach, and a multi-millionaire. It is no exaggeration to say that without the lessons I learned about leading from the trenches, taking care of people, and focusing on others, I wouldn't be where I am today—and you wouldn't be reading this book.

After I left the service, I became a pilot and an engineer. Those experiences made me a meticulous planner, which was also foundationally important to my success. To be successful in life—to build empires—we can't shoot from the hip. We can't wake up every day without any idea about where we want to go and expect to get anywhere meaningful. We need some type of strategic plan, some way of keeping score. The key to all of that is becoming meticulous about planning.

To see why, let's pretend for a moment that I told you to get in your car and drive. I don't give you a destination. I just tell you to hop in, start the ignition, and go. What do you do? Most likely, you get in your car and start driving around in circles. You waste gas, you waste time, and you don't go anywhere meaningful, right?

Unfortunately, this parallels how most people approach their business lives. That's one of the reasons so many businesses fail within their first one, five, or ten years! People start their "road trip" without a specific, concrete destination in mind.

Now, let's change the game a little bit. Imagine that I tell you I want you to drive from Los Angeles to New York City. Suddenly, you have a destination. That means you can plan your route. You can figure out where to eat and sleep. You can pick out milestones along the way, and you can determine exactly how long it will take you to reach each one. By simply defining a destination, we just astronomically increased your chances of reaching your goal efficiently and successfully.

Similarly, when launching a business, start by determining your destination. Once you've identified your end point, you can create your plan, or your road map, for exactly how you'll get there.

Being a pilot and an engineer taught me to start with the end in mind. Pilots don't take off without knowing where they're going, what the winds are, and what the weather en route is. Pilots spend a lot of time thinking about all the different variables at play before we ever get into the cockpit. Indeed, for a pilot, planning is the difference between success and failure. The same holds true for engineers. When we're building something, we create a process first. We outline, define the plan, and then work through each step, one by one, until we achieve our goal.

Thanks to my pilot training and my engineering experience, I learned early on that planning is critical to every part of life. Add that skill set to what I learned in the army, and the result is a servant leader who cares about people and understands how to plan for success.

LEARNING FROM THE BEST

Now, add in another key experience: my time at General Electric (GE) during the Camelot era. Jack Welch was the CEO, and under his watch, GE was arguably the world's most admired company. With Jack at the helm, GE was growing so fast that its stock was splitting every three years. And that's where I, the young servant leader and meticulous planner, learned how empires are built and run.

After an incredible decade-long career at GE, I spent twenty-one years as the CEO of three different national companies. During that time, I ran companies for nine different private equity sponsors, and I completed fifty-eight acquisitions—which directly translated to billions of dollars in successful exits.

It wasn't long before I became known in private equity circles as a "turnaround guy." In other words, I took over underperforming businesses as a CEO, and by rebuilding and rebranding them, I got them scaling again, often to the tune of a sustained 30 percent compound annual growth rate (CAGR). And I did it over and over, in multiple industries.

I had no experience in any of my companies' industries before I started. But I had my foundational toolkit—servant leadership, meticulous planning, and the strategies I learned from leaders like Jack Welch—and I was able to use those tools to turn every company I ran into a bona fide empire.

Fast forward to today. I serve on the boards of multiple large companies. I coach dozens of founders and entrepreneurs to grow their own businesses. I work with private equity firms, their portfolio companies, and CEOs. And once again, in almost every instance, I have not had industry experience for any of the companies I'm involved with. But that doesn't matter. Using my foundational skills and the exact tools I'll share with you in this book, I've been able to bend the growth curve of all these different companies and help turn them into empires.

That's what I want to teach you to do, too.

WHAT WE'LL COVER

This book is about how to build an empire. Along the way, you'll learn everything you need to know to take your business as far as you want to go—even if you're starting from zero and want to grow to a billion dollars. It will touch on some of the same subjects that I discussed in my first two books, but my goal here is to look at those topics through a different lens.

To quickly recap, my first book, *The Private Equity Playbook*, educates business owners and entrepreneurs about private equity (which is now one of the world's largest economic forces). Collectively, private equity has more than $5 trillion at play, and it is responsible for buying and selling over 50 percent of all businesses on the planet. While we won't do a deep dive into private equity here, we will talk about it and how you may be able to use it to help build your empire.

My second book, *The Exit Strategy Playbook*, is about entrepreneurs and their exit paths. It includes some aspects of private equity, but it also covers the broader universe of potential buyers and how entrepreneurs can maximize the potential of their business exit. We will touch on exiting your business in this book, but only as it relates to building your empire (so if you want to learn about exits in-depth, I recommend reading *The Exit Strategy Playbook*).

Back to *Empire Builder*. It is a detailed guide—a road map, if you will—that lays out, step by step, exactly what you need to do to turn your business into an empire. I've organized it into four sections, with each building on the previous one.

Section 1 sets the stage by discussing the importance of culture to your business. Importantly, this section also describes the four stages of growth and offers a primer on private equity.

Section 2 covers the foundational basics you must understand to start to bend your growth curve up and transform your business.

Once you have the basics dialed in, we shift our attention in section 3 to more advanced tools you can use to continue scaling your business toward the billion-dollar mark.

Finally, in section 4, we talk about monetizing your asset and maximizing the economic potential of your business. This is also where we tie everything together, and you get the final tools you need to build your empire.

IT'S TIME TO TAKE ACTION

Make no mistake—this is a book of action. It doesn't include a study of business theory or a bunch of case studies I've simply read about and am commenting on. Bottom line, I'm not approaching building an empire from an academic perspective.

Everything you read in these pages is drawn from real-life experience. The strategies I share are all based on proven results, and they all come from what I've learned first-hand, what I've learned in my time working with private equity, and what I've learned over the years from coaching entrepreneurs just like you.

So, what do you say? Are you ready to get started? Then let's dive in.

ONE

BUILD WHAT YOU KNOW

T HE GREAT WARREN BUFFETT—THE ORACLE OF Omaha—is often quoted as saying, "Never invest in something you don't understand." It's fantastic advice, but because I like to put a positive spin on things when I'm talking with investors, entrepreneurs, and founders, I say it in a slightly different way: *Invest in what you know.*

How does this relate to empire building? To answer that, let me begin by giving you an example of how I've applied this approach to great effect in my own life.

Let's go back some years to when I first heard the great man's advice. Buffett was talking about figuring out what businesses to invest in, remember, so I spent some time thinking about the companies I know and use on a daily basis. Almost immediately, five came to mind: Apple, Amazon, Microsoft, Google, and The Home Depot.

All of my devices are made by Apple. Amazon comes to my house (and my neighbors' houses) almost every day. Almost all businesses use Microsoft applications. Everyone has a Gmail account and watches YouTube. And, I go to Home Depot regularly, because I'm always working on projects around the house.

Once I had a list of companies I knew, I put Buffett's advice to the test. I invested $100,000 in each of those five stocks, for a total investment of $500,000. Five years later, my return was an impressive $2,500,000.

BUILD WHAT YOU KNOW PEOPLE NEED

A return of 5X multiple of invested capital (MOIC) in just five years is a pretty good result, wouldn't you say? And here's the best part: this advice doesn't just work for picking stocks. If you learn to apply it to your business, it can also help you build your empire.

To show you what I mean, let's tweak the advice again, just slightly. Instead of *invest in what you know*, let's change it to *build what you know people need*. The world over, people have certain universal needs. They need a place to live. They need their roofs fixed. They need clean drinking water and medical services. In the developed world, people need auto insurance, well-maintained yards, food for their pets, and dental cleanings. And these things are the tip of the iceberg; the list of needs is truly vast.

Along with needs, people also have certain wants. They want security cameras. They want new, energy-efficient windows for their houses. They want new outfits, accessories for their cars, and bigger TVs. Sure, they may want these things badly, but at the end of the day, they don't need any of them.

Here's why this matters: when the economy is bad, people may slow down or delay spending for their needs, but they won't stop buying needed products and services altogether. But if a product or service is discretionary—if it's a want—then people may very well elect to forgo that expense (sometimes indefinitely) in a recession or a down economy.

With that in mind, go back to the advice I just shared. When you're building an empire, focus on servicing needs, not wants. That's the only way to build a business that's sustainable and scalable no matter what's happening in the world around you.

INSULATE YOURSELF FROM DOWNTURNS

Like the stock market, our economy goes in cycles. Sometimes, it's in a period of expansion. Inevitably, though, it will reach a peak and start to come back down. Any number of things can cause a downturn: a pandemic, a housing crisis, inflation, a war—the list goes on and on. If things go too far, we may enter a recession (or even a depression). Eventually, though, the economy will hit a bottom and start to recover, or expand, until it hits a peak and goes down again. These cycles are inevitable. But by focusing on fulfilling needs, you can insulate yourself from downturns. In other words, you can build resilience into your business—which is a prerequisite for building an empire.

Let me give you a real-life example of this. I was the CEO of a large North American commercial laundry company, WASH Multifamily Laundry Systems. We had 600,000 coin-operated washing machines in 70,000 locations (primarily apartment complexes) throughout two countries. During the Great Recession of 2008 and 2009, when people were getting laid off in large numbers, our business was impacted. Unemployed people, it turns out, don't do as much laundry as employed people.

Ultimately, though, everybody still has to do laundry whether they are employed or not. We were serving a need, not a want, and because of that all-important fact, our "peak to trough" (the difference between our revenue when the economy was at its peak versus when it bottomed out) was only 8 percent. Not only that—when the economy turned around, we were able to recover to pre-recession revenue levels incredibly rapidly.

This example illustrates the value of serving needs. But there's another benefit to focusing on needs over wants— and as an empire builder, this benefit should be just as important to you. Eventually, you will sell your company (more about this in section 4), and buyers will pay far more for a business that's recession-resistant than they will for one that gets hammered every time the economy goes down. Put another way, if buyers can see that your business services *needs* (not wants), they will value your company far more highly.

WHAT TO FOCUS ON IN A SERVICE BUSINESS

Now that you understand why it's so important to focus on needs in any business you build (or acquire), I want to go a step further and explore how to apply this advice to your specific type of business. First, let's consider service-based businesses. Whether you are building or buying, you already know that a service business should fulfill a need. Beyond that, though, it should also be in a highly fragmented industry. I call this "passing the phonebook test."

Pretend there's a stack of different phonebooks sitting in front of you. For the purposes of this example, let's say you open each one to the "landscape maintenance" category. If you can find the names of different landscape maintenance companies for each city in each different phonebook, it's a highly fragmented market—and a highly fragmented market is ripe for empire building. This is similar to a buyer's market versus a seller's market in real estate. In a buyer's market (i.e., a fragmented industry), there's a large amount of inventory. Prices are lower, and buyers can be choosy. In a seller's market, though (which is the equivalent of a non-fragmented industry), the lack of inventory means prices get driven up and buyers can't be as picky. Stay away from a seller's market (i.e., a non-fragmented industry) if you can!

Why do you want a fragmented market? It all comes down to a strategy known as "buy-and-build." We'll dive more into this concept in chapter 8, but the bottom line is that, if you're in a fragmented market, not only will you be able to buy smaller companies to bolster your empire more cheaply, but when you sell your bigger company, the multiple you will be able to sell it for will be much higher (we'll talk about this in more detail in chapter 4).

So, that's two pieces of the service-based business puzzle: a focus on needs, and a highly fragmented industry. The third piece of the puzzle is recurrent revenue streams. Let's stick with the landscape maintenance business example. People need their grass cut every week, so that's the core *recurrent* service the business offers. You can sign ongoing maintenance contracts with your customers and get consistent revenue for relatively little capital. All you need, after all, is a truck, some tools, and people to operate the mowers, weed whackers, and blowers.

The final piece of the service-based business puzzle is low (or medium) complexity. If you can fill a need in a highly fragmented industry that has the potential for recurrent revenue streams with low or semi-skilled labor, you've found the golden ticket. Landscape maintenance businesses, janitorial or maid service companies, and most home services companies all fall into this category, and therefore, they are good candidates for empire building.

WHAT TO FOCUS ON IN A REAL ESTATE BUSINESS

If you have a real estate business, things look a little different. You should still focus on needs (single-family homes and apartment complexes rather than commercial office space, for example, since the number of people working out of an office is rapidly declining). Beyond that, I recommend laying the foundation for your empire by focusing on one particular segment of real estate. That means investing *only* in single-family homes *or* only in apartment complexes—not trying to focus on both at the same time.

Once you've narrowed your focus down to a single segment, invest in an area you know, such as your own city. You recognize good and bad neighborhoods in your area. You know the desirable places with high rental demands. And, you are aware of the places to avoid because of high crime or other issues. Leverage that knowledge; it will pay off handsomely as you build your empire.

As you get more experience, you can invest in additional markets and segments. Initially, though, stay focused on one type of real estate, and keep to areas you know like the back of your hand.

WHAT TO FOCUS ON IN A PRODUCT BUSINESS

What if you're buying or building a product-based business? You already know what I'm going to say: start by focusing on needs. Beyond that, though, it's crucial that your product-based business is highly adaptable and fluid, so it can keep up with consumers' constantly shifting demands. There are a few steps to achieving this.

First, a good product-based business should have a high-margin profile. We'll get more into margin and how to enhance it in chapter 7, but for now, a good rule of thumb is that the margin on the products being sold must be high enough to sustain overhead and generate consistent profit.

Next, make sure you build or buy a business that has a family of products that fill a recurrent need. Let me give you an example. Many of us have pets, so we need to buy pet food. But while someone is buying your pet food, they may also buy pet toys and pet supplements. The idea is to think of your offerings in terms of a core product and adjacent ancillary items that also fulfill a need for your customers.

A strong product-based business that can help you build your empire should also be what I call "manufacturing- and inventory-light." Manufacturing and storing inventory requires a lot of capital expenditure and overhead, so look for (or build) a business that sells products someone else makes and dropships to customers directly from the manufacturer's warehouse. A great example of this kind of business may be one that operates as a third-party seller on Amazon. It doesn't have to manufacture or store any inventory; instead, customers order products made by the manufacturer, Amazon sends their order directly to them, and you get paid.

Finally, a good product-based business should have a strong online presence. Consumer habits are shifting, and people are buying more and more products online. (As a side note, nearly one out of three businesses don't have a website. In your journey to build an empire, an effective website and e-commerce engine—particularly if you sell products—is a must.)

IT'S TIME TO START YOUR EMPIRE

Now that we've set the stage, it's time to turn our attention to starting your empire. There are two ways to do this: build your own business from scratch, or buy a pre-existing business to serve as your platform for growth. Remember, whichever you choose, you need to focus on needs, not wants, and you need to make sure the business you buy or build meets the specific criteria I laid out for the type of business (e.g., service, real estate, or product).

You can absolutely build a business from scratch. However, there is a risk to doing that: you don't know when you start out whether or not you will be successful. We are going to talk a lot about how to maximize your potential for success in the next chapter, but still, the risks are there.

If you buy a pre-existing business, your risk drops. You can see how healthy it is. You can see whether it has customers and what its revenue is. You can look at its history and financials. Bottom line, there is plenty of information available to analyze whether it's a strong platform from which to begin your empire.

There are many online tools you can use to research all manner of information about potential businesses within any given market. One of my favorites is Grata. PrivSource and PitchBook are also excellent. These tools can be expensive (at the time of this writing, for example, Grata is $10,000 per year), but if you are searching for a business to acquire, they are often worthwhile investments.

I personally prefer to find proprietary deals. That means I do my research on the industry I'm interested in and develop an investment thesis (in a nutshell, an investment thesis is an objective, research-based argument for a particular investment strategy, which can be used as a strategic decision-making tool). Next, I identify the ideal target profile of the type of company I'm looking for. My target profile might include revenue size, earnings size, specific geographic markets served, and specific customer verticals. From there, I start building a funnel of potential targets. Then, I reach out to owners to further develop my initial targets. I have found this approach to be very effective, but it is far from the only way to find potential companies from which to grow your empire. We will discuss more strategies in chapter 8.

FINDING THE MONEY

Whether you decide to buy a company or build one from scratch, inevitably, you will reach a point where you need funds. Luckily, you have a few options for obtaining the money you need. First, you can use cash. If you don't have enough cash yourself, you can bring in partners—family, friends, and/or people you know from the business world— and leverage their capital.

The second source of money is a commercial bank. Most large financial institutions (particularly the national banks: Wells Fargo, Chase, or Bank of America) have commercial banking. If you already have an existing relationship with one of these large banks, you may be able to secure better terms, so talk to them about obtaining a business loan. If you don't, spend some time researching the terms offered by various commercial banks, then work with the most favorable to try and secure a loan.

If you are in the United States, you can also go to the Small Business Administration (if you aren't in the US, seek out your country's small business agency and ask them what business loans or grants they offer). If you are purchasing a business, you can ask the seller to roll over some of their equity into the business you are going to build. You can also ask them to finance your purchase by holding back a note at a specific interest rate.

Another option I have used to great effect is to work with a private equity group. Many private equity firms back people who are planning to buy and run businesses, which makes them good candidates for helping you fund your empire (more about private equity in chapter 4).

A REAL-LIFE EXAMPLE:
FINANCING AN INSURANCE AGENCY

Sometimes, the best approach is to use a combination of the methods I described above. My brother and I, for example, once bought an insurance agency (and yes, it ticked all the boxes: it serviced needs, it was in an industry that passed the phone-book test, it had recurrent revenue streams, and it was medium complexity). We paid $4 million for it.

To finance the $4 million, we borrowed $1 million from the seller at a 10 percent interest rate. We borrowed $2 million from a family office (a form of private equity). Then, we brought in three friends and came up with the remaining $1 million between the five of us. In total, we used $1 million of equity and $3 million in debt.

The business generated $1.7 million per year in cash flow, and from that, we were able to pay off the cost of acquiring it within four years. We ran the business for about fifteen years, then sold it for $12 million. While these numbers are not huge when compared to some empires I have built, in terms of MOIC, it was the single best investment of my career when considering equity investment, distributions made while owning, and the final sale price at exit.

Bottom line, there are a lot of different ways to raise the capital needed to buy or build your company. Remember, too, whether you buy or build doesn't really matter; there are pros and cons to each. What *is* important is ensuring the business you buy or build meets the foundational empire-building criteria we discussed throughout this chapter.

KEY TAKEAWAYS

- Building a business is like investing in the stock market: go with what you know.
- No matter what kind of business you have, focus on creating offerings that fulfill people's needs.
- The ideal service-based business is highly fragmented with recurrent revenue streams and low (or medium) complexity.

- When investing in real estate, focus on a single segment close to where you live.
- Product-based businesses should have high-margin profiles, offer families of products, be manufacturing- and inventory-lite, and have a strong online presence.
- When you begin building your empire, you can choose to either build a business from scratch or buy a pre-existing business. Whichever option you choose, there are many ways to obtain the financing you will need.

TWO

FRAMING THE BASE OF YOUR EMPIRE

OW YOU UNDERSTAND THE IMPORTANCE OF *building what you know*—whether you're buying a business you plan to make into an empire, building one from scratch, or focusing on a business you already have. Let's continue our empire-building journey by talking about some of the overarching themes I've learned over the past thirty-five years. Think of these as the frame of your empire. You must master them before you can take your business to the heights you initially dreamed of, so it's worth spending some time unpacking them here.

The first (and arguably the most important) of these themes is that culture and revenue are directly correlated. The second theme: before you can build an empire, you must become a magnet in your industry. Third, your leadership attitude matters. Fourth, to the greatest extent possible, you must maintain transparency with your people at all times. And finally, you must be data-driven; that is key to measuring success at every single level.

MANAGE FOR CULTURE, NOT REVENUE

Many entrepreneurs—and CEOS, for that matter—are primarily focused on revenue. This is understandable, but also incorrect. In business, you cannot manage revenue from the top down. You can only control revenue by building culture from the ground up.

This is crucial to understand, so let me say it another way. If you focus solely on revenue, you are missing the point. Yes, you need to be aware that you have revenue. You also need to be aware of what your revenue is. However, your job as a leader is *not* to manage revenue. It is to build a strong culture. If this runs counter to what you've been taught in the past, it may help to think of it this way:

revenue is the outcome of the business that you are running, and in my experience, all business starts with culture. When you build a strong culture, you will create an engaged workforce.

Think about it for a moment. Most of the time, people generally enjoy what they do for a living. But, they want to have a voice. They want to be treated fairly and with respect. They must believe their leaders value what they think. And, they need to feel like they are part of something greater than themselves. Achieving all of this comes down to culture.

When you have a culture that makes your employees feel valued, they will be engaged. An engaged workforce automatically takes great care of your customers. Customers reward that engagement by giving your company more work—and as a result, revenue rains from the skies. And guess what? This is true whether you have a service-based business, a product-based business, or a real estate business. It's also true whether you have two employees or 2,000. In every instance, a strong culture leads to strong revenue.

If, on the other hand, you have a toxic culture, your employees will disengage. They may leave altogether, and even if they stay, they certainly won't take good care of your customers with any kind of consistency. A weak, toxic culture will never lead to a highly performing business. It won't allow you to maximize the potential of your organization. And, it certainly won't allow you to build an empire.

BECOME A MAGNET EMPLOYER

So, how do you build a strong culture and an engaged workforce? Simple: you make it your goal to create an environment where people want to (and can) spend their entire careers. In other words, you must become the magnet in your industry—the employer of choice.

Aim to become a multi-generational employer, too. Make it your mission to build a business where fathers talk to their sons about the value of working at your company. When daughters graduate from high school, they should eagerly come work for you, alongside their mothers or aunts or cousins.

If you're like many entrepreneurs I talk to, you may be thinking this goal sounds good, but that it's unrealistic. After all, we're living in the age of Quiet Quitting. The Great Resignation is still fresh in our minds. But here's the thing: if you are the employer of choice in an industry—if you are the magnet—talent will come to you, and it will stay with you. It's your job to manage the culture so that it does.

Accomplishing this doesn't need to be complicated. In fact, you can achieve it by implementing what I call the four-legged stool (comprised of fair wages, excellent benefits, strong retirement options, and opportunities for growth). For the first leg of the stool: pay a fair wage. If you don't, you will lose talent. Second leg: provide excellent benefits to *all* your people. Remember, you want your people to stay with you for their entire careers, which means you need to help take care of them as they get older. So, give the person cleaning the floors and the guy driving the truck the same benefits package your top leadership gets. This is foundational to becoming a magnet.

The third leg of the stool is to get a strong retirement plan in place. Experts predict that, in less than fifteen years, Social Security may not be able to fully pay benefits. People know this, and they are increasingly looking to their employers to provide a viable solution. To the greatest extent you can, then, create as rich a retirement plan as possible. For example, when you set up your 401k plans, rather than offering 50 cents on the dollar up to 6 percent, consider matching employee contributions dollar for dollar up to 3 percent. That sort of math makes sense to people and demonstrates that you understand they may not be able to afford to give up 6 percent of their salary and still pay the bills, *but you are committed to taking care of them anyway*. Remember: take care of your people, and they will take care of your customers—and ultimately, you.

Create Opportunities for Growth

Even if you get the first three legs right, unless you have the final leg firmly in place, your stool is going to topple. If that happens, you will lose people. That's why you need the last, most important leg: creating opportunities for growth.

As you work to build your empire, your company will get larger and larger. That growth creates the fuel and opportunity for your people to advance in their careers. Let's say you run a service business. To be successful, there's no question you need the people who have contentedly spent the last twenty years doing the same job, day in and day out. They are the experts who will teach the next generation of employees how to do the job and do it well. They are, in fact, part of your intellectual property and part of your foundation for success.

At the same time, you also need the people who are doing a job today, but dream of one day becoming service managers, regional managers, or vice presidents. How do I know? *Because I'm that guy.* Thirty-five years ago, I was in that truck, working as a technician at hospitals for GE, dreaming of becoming a manager and, eventually, a CEO. I was hungry for growth, and if my leadership hadn't provided me with opportunities for advancement, I would have quickly left to find a company that would.

This doesn't mean you force people to climb the corporate ladder. Just providing the opportunity is enough (and by the way, a company with strong growth is a company that's expanding, and that expansion creates advancement opportunities).

Keep in mind, too, that you must be strategic about advancement opportunities. It's incumbent on us as empire builders to make sure our people are prepared for promotion. Remember, culture and revenue are correlated. When you promote someone to a leadership position, you are effectively putting them in charge of your most important product: your employees. So, make your first-time leaders go through leadership training so they don't make mistakes that will drive off your talent!

I see it over and over again: entrepreneurs don't want to spend money training their first-line supervisors and other management. Avoid making this mistake. If leadership is inept or toxic, your stool will tumble, and your most valuable asset—your people—will leave.

One of the companies I turned around was struggling with turnover. When I walked in the door for the first time, the company's annual turnover rate was a whopping 42 percent. There's no way anyone can build an empire when almost half of their employees are leaving every single year. So, we set about building our four-legged stool.

Within twelve months, we reduced voluntary turnover by more than 50 percent. In eighteen months, we had cut it down to the teens, which was the lowest it had been in decades. What makes this especially meaningful is that this was a trade-based business, and in trade-based businesses, turnover is generally much higher. But, by applying the principles I've shared with you here, intentionally and consistently, we were able to drastically reduce turnover almost immediately.

Reduce, or Even Eliminate, Turnover

The four-legged stool is all about reducing turnover. In today's world, this goal is more important than ever. There's a shortage of workers, and everybody's competing for talent. Your job as an empire builder is to build a sustainable business where you can easily attract and retain the very best people. Paying a fair wage, offering excellent benefits, providing a solid retirement plan, and creating opportunities for advancement are the keys to doing that.

LEADERSHIP ATTITUDE MATTERS

Culture is also deeply impacted by leadership's attitude. In every company I run, I have a mantra that I repeat to my leadership: *you don't get to have a bad day.* Remember, your leaders are managing your product (which, as you now know, is your employees). Encourage them to bring their problems to you or other senior leadership if they need help, but make it clear that they cannot take their bad days out on your people.

A good leadership attitude also means being transparent. I learned this lesson early, while I was in the military. Over and over, my commanding officers approached goals with complete transparency. They told us what our mission was, how we were going to achieve it, and why it was important. All the great leaders I have since worked with have mirrored this approach.

So, as much as possible when you're building your empire, stay away from secrets. Of course, if you have a nondisclosure agreement (NDA) or some legal reason to keep a secret, you have to honor that. But except for those rare exceptions, make it a point to have regular, open dialogue with your employees. If you want their buy-in and loyalty, they have to know everything you know. Just as importantly, they have to *believe* you will always be transparent and open with them.

Let me be clear here: being transparent isn't about forcing the consumption of information. It's about making information accessible, so your people feel supported and included whether they participate or not. When I ran a company with more than 3,000 employees, I would hold regular town halls. I would talk about revenue, EBITDA (earnings before interest, taxes, depreciation, and amortization), our financial goals and objectives, and more. Each town hall saw well over a thousand people tuning in live. We also recorded it so that others could listen later if they chose to.

Think back to our proverbial road trip. When you start on the journey to building an empire, you can't keep everyone else in the dark when it comes to your destination. And, you can't hide the route you're going to take. After all, you can't drive the car to the destination by yourself—it's too far away. Give your people the road map, too, and keep them up to date on everything that's happening, so they can support you on your journey.

MEASURE SUCCESS
AT EVERY LEVEL

As you work toward becoming a best-in-class company—which is foundational to building your empire—remember that culture is directly correlated to revenue. Support your culture by implementing the four-legged stool. Manage your attitude and be transparent.

Finally, learn to measure success at every level. This requires implementing metrics for all your people *and* making sure they understand how their metrics build up into higher-level metrics that govern the health and productivity of the company. After all, a financially healthy company leads to benefits for them, too.

Take the guy driving the truck to service calls, for example. When he hits his metrics, it supports your ability to buy him a new truck and better equipment. It allows you to invest in technology that will enable him to do high-value work instead of repetitive, low-value tasks. It lets you send him to training so he can move up the corporate ladder. All of those things are only possible if that guy (along with everyone else) nails their metrics, so be data-driven. Be transparent about what you're measuring, how well it's being achieved, and how it impacts your people.

These steps set the stage for your empire's frame.

Since you now understand what goes into a solid business upon which to build your empire, it's time to dig into the stages of growth. In the next chapter, I'll show you how to hit the ground running with your startup and grow it from $0 in revenue to $1 million, $10 million, $100 million, and finally, $1 billion dollars.

KEY TAKEAWAYS

- Culture and revenue are directly correlated. Build a strong culture, and strong revenue will follow.

- Use the concept of the four-legged stool to create a best-in-class company that attracts and retains top talent.
- Attitude matters. As a leader, you don't get to have a bad day, and neither do the rest of your leadership team.
- Unless you are prohibited by a nondisclosure agreement, refrain from keeping secrets from your workforce. Your goal should always be complete transparency.
- Measure success at every level. Make sure your people understand how their success contributes to the overall success of the company, and how that success, in turn, will come back to them.

THREE

GOING FROM STARTUP TO EMPIRE

YOU MAY REMEMBER FROM THE INTRODUCTION that there are about 33 million small businesses in the United States. Collectively, these businesses employ half the American workforce. And yet—as we also talked about in the introduction—as numerous as they are, only about 7 percent of small businesses have a revenue of $1 million or more. Even worse, more than 50 percent fail in their first five years.

As troubling as these numbers are, as someone who has built multiple successful companies and had billions of dollars in successful exits, I can say beyond a shadow of a doubt that they do not mean *your* business is doomed to failure. You absolutely can achieve success, as long as you get certain key things right at each stage of your business's growth.

STAGE 1: $0 TO $1 MILLION

I'm going to let you in on a secret: there's really only one reason why 93 percent of small businesses never reach $1 million in revenue. And no, it isn't because their founders lack the desire and drive to achieve success. Truthfully, in almost every instance, the reason a small business struggles is that the entrepreneur or small business owner fails to get their *unit-level economics* right. (This term refers to your specific business's revenues and costs as they relate to an individual unit.) And that brings us to another secret: if you want to build a billion-dollar business—and ultimately, an empire—first you have to build the perfect million-dollar business. No, scratch that: first you have to build the perfect *hundred-thousand-dollar* business. In other words, your business needs to work at the smallest unit level possible before you even *think* about scaling.

I can't tell you how many times I've heard entrepreneurs say, "I'll figure out how to be profitable once I'm bigger." That's the mindset that gets small business owners into trouble. Get it right small—or walk away early, before you waste valuable time, money, and effort on a losing proposition.

If you aren't sure how to do that, don't worry. We're going to walk through how to check your unit-level economics right now. For the purposes of example, we'll use a landscape maintenance company, but the concept holds true for every kind of business in every kind of industry and every geographic market.

Build Your Mathematical Formula for Success

The first step to getting your unit-level economics right is to *identify what they are.* In our mythical landscape maintenance business, the unit-level economics are the monthly payment, fuel costs, insurance costs, and maintenance reserves for one truck, one fully burdened (includes wages and benefits) two-person crew, and the operating costs of the equipment necessary to maintain your customers' lawns: a commercial lawnmower, a blower, a weed whacker, some rakes, shovels, and so on. For the sake of illustrating how to build the operating expenses formula, we are going to use some lightly researched numbers:

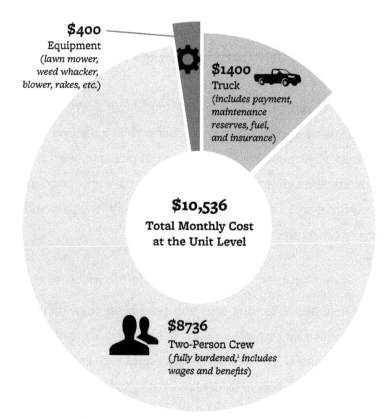

$400
Equipment
(lawn mower, weed whacker, blower, rakes, etc.)

$1400
Truck
(includes payment, maintenance reserves, fuel, and insurance)

$10,536
Total Monthly Cost
at the Unit Level

$8736
Two-Person Crew
(fully burdened,[1] includes wages and benefits)

---

1   Fully burdened employee costs include hourly wages (or salaries) plus all additional costs, such as taxes, benefits, and supplies. Essentially, you can think of the fully burdened labor cost as the total hourly cost to employ someone for the hours they work.

Now that we've identified those, we can build a mathematical formula for success. This formula is specifically focused on revenue and direct operating costs; it does not include capital expenditures or Sales and General Administration (SG&A) costs—we'll factor those in later. (As a side note, spend some time researching any unfamiliar terms. Building an empire requires that you understand these and other basics of financial statements.)

Add these numbers up, and you get your unit-level direct operating expenses: $10,536/month, or $126,432/year. Now, you need to ask yourself a question: *Can I bring in enough revenue to cover my direct operating expenses while leaving enough gross profit to cover overhead and generate the minimum acceptable net profit?*

Again, let's use some lightly researched numbers to explore how you can find the answer to that question. A typical crew can cut 15 lawns per day, at $50 per cut. Assuming an average of about 22 cutting days per month, the average monthly revenue per crew is approximately $16,500, and the average annual revenue per crew is approximately $198,000. A quick note: here in Texas, lawns are cut year-round. In northern climates where lawns aren't cut in the winter, most landscape maintenance businesses perform services such as snow removal, winterizing irrigation systems, and putting up holiday lighting to bridge the seasonal reduction in lawn-cutting work. For illustrative purposes and simplicity, this example assumes a warm climate where lawns are cut throughout the year.

Subtract the annual unit-level direct operating cost ($126,432) from the annual average gross revenue ($198,000) to get the annual gross operating profit per crew. The answer: $71,568, or 36 percent. Now, deduct the SG&A (which includes your costs to manage the business, get customers, pay yourself, and so on). It should never be more than 20 percent, so let's assume 20 percent, which will leave you with 16 percent in pretax net profit. The minimum pretax net profit percentage a business must achieve to be viable is 10 percent, so in this example, the unit-level economics seem to work.

Of course, there are a lot of variable costs built into this formula. The cost of gasoline, insurance, and labor costs can go up, for example. So can the cost to service and operate your equipment. The revenue you can get per lawn can fluctuate, too, as can the number of lawns your crew can cut each day. You also need to account for bad weather days or times when a worker calls in sick. All of these scenarios mean you need to be very diligent about monitoring your variable costs to ensure your unit-level economics remain sound. But ultimately, by getting the variables right and tracking the basic economics of your business at the very smallest level—in this case, the economics of running a business with one crew—you create the foundation from which you can build an empire.

Once you've perfected your operating formula, you can determine exactly how to scale to $1 million. Let me show you how to do this using the same numbers we came up with initially. Take your revenue goal ($1 million), and divide it by your annual revenue per crew ($198,000). That calculation returns an answer of 5.05, but since you can't buy 0.5 of a truck or hire 0.5 of a crew, let's round up to 6. So, you need 6 trucks and 12 employees to hit your revenue target.

Six trucks and 12 employees will bring in about $1,188,000 in revenue; $427,680 in gross profit; and $190,080 in pretax net profit. To hit your revenue targets, you will need 450 regular weekly customers.

Again, these numbers are just to illustrate the fundamental concept. The bottom line is that success is tied to your unit-level economics. Get your formula right at the smallest level, and you will be well on your way to ensuring your small business is one of the 7 percent that reach the million-dollar milestone. Get it wrong, though—or fail to consider it at all because you assume profitability is tied to how big your business is—and chances are high your company will become one of the scary statistics I laid out in the introduction.

Find Your Capital Costs

At this point, you may be wondering where your capital expenditures come in. They're definitely important, so let's dig into them a little bit.

Let's assume you can buy a landscape truck for $60,000. Six trucks, then, will cost $360,000. You put 30 percent down on each truck, or $108,000 total. The monthly payment for the financed portion of the truck is included in your monthly truck operating costs. The capital cost is merely the down payment required to buy each truck. Six commercial lawnmowers will cost you $36,000; you will buy those outright. You also need 6 blowers, 6 weed whackers, and 6 sets of hand tools; assume a total of $6,000 for all of those (also bought outright). Add those numbers up, and your total capital cost to build a million-dollar landscape maintenance business is $150,000.

You already know from chapter 1 that there are plenty of places to get this money. You could use cash, get capital from family or friends, get a commercial business loan, and so on. Regardless, at this point, you have the basic information you need about both operating expenses and capital expenses to decide whether or not to move forward or walk away—and in this example, the unit-level economics look pretty good. To be absolutely sure of that, you can check your numbers against the *30, 20, and 10 rule*, where 30 percent is the minimum gross profit, 20 percent is the maximum sg&a spend, and 10 percent is the minimum net profit. (Remember to research any terms that are unfamiliar to you.)

Identify the Make-or-Break Issues

Before you pull the trigger on starting your landscaping business, there are a few other things you need to think about. Perhaps the most important of these considerations are what I call the *make-or-break issues*. What are the factors that mean the difference between success and failure for this stage of your business?

In our landscaping business example, the first make-or-break issue in reaching the million-dollar threshold is whether or not you can find 450 regular weekly customers. If you can't, you won't be able to reach your revenue target, which means customer acquisition (and the cost of acquiring customers) will be a key component of your success. Another make-or-break issue is density. Having clusters of customers that are close to each other geographically will increase your crews' productivity and decrease your vehicle operating costs. Landscape company owners with density have told me their crews can cut up to twenty lawns per day. I used fifteen in our example, simply for illustrative purposes and to create a hedge against those days when the weather is bad or you're scrambling to deal with staffing issues. Ultimately, though, more lawns (or larger lawns) equals more revenue—and since density is key to driving efficiency, it's certainly another make-or-break issue.

Make-or-break issues can differ for each business, so you'll need to do your homework to determine those specific to you. That means spending time researching your industry, reviewing your unit-level economics, and maybe even talking to a coach or peer group to get a sense of which factors will make the difference between your business's success and failure. It may take some time to do all this, but don't skip this step: getting your operating formula and make-or-break issues dialed in is crucial. When you get these factors right, you build a company that has consistent revenue, margin, and earnings that provide stability from the get-go. Not only that, but you also build a company that will become an asset you can later sell for a multiple of earnings.

Ultimately, the most important thing to keep in mind in this first stage is that to successfully build a large business (and an empire), you must start by building a successful small business. Don't worry about growth when you're starting out—worry about truly understanding your unit-level operating costs, your average revenue, your make-or-break issues, and your capital expenditures. Pre-launch, these assumptions help drive your business plan. When acquiring an existing business, they inform your early understanding of how the business works. Get them in order, and you will be set up for massive future success.

STAGE 2: $1 MILLION TO $10 MILLION

Once you've reached the million-dollar mark, you've done the heavy lifting. To scale from $1 million to $10 million, then, all you really need to do is *replicate* the same success that took you to the million-dollar threshold.

Let's go back to our landscape business so you can see how this works. Remember that the average annual revenue per crew is $198,000. Just as you did to reach $1 million, divide your revenue by your goal ($10 million). When you do, you will see that you need 51 trucks and 102 employees. Fifty-one crews will give you $10.098 million in annual revenue, $3.635 million in gross profit, and $1.616 million in pretax net profit. You will need 3,825 weekly customers to reach these targets.

The make-or-break issue here is whether or not you will be able to increase your weekly customers from 450 to 3,825. However, at this stage, if you are in a densely populated Metropolitan Statistical Area (MSA), you can generally find all the customers you need within your base market.

To further bolster your revenue, you can also start to offer ancillary services. For example, you might offer lawn fertilization services, sprinkler repair, tree trimming, bed mulching, landscape lighting, holiday lighting, and so on. By upselling these ancillary services to your existing customers—after, of course, making sure the unit-level economics are right—you can more quickly grow your business to $10 million.

Finally, this is often the stage where you can begin to take advantage of what's known as operating leverage. We'll discuss this strategy more in chapter 7, but for now, suffice it to say that as you get bigger, your purchasing volume increases. Instead of buying just 1 truck, or even buying 6, at this stage, you'll be buying 51 trucks. Because you're buying in volume, you'll get a better price for each of those 51 trucks than you would if you were buying a smaller number. That's operating leverage in action, and you can use it to drive down costs and enhance your margins.

Wondering about your capital expenditures? Use the same formula as you did to determine your capital costs in Stage 1, but this time, plug in 51 trucks, not 6. Remember, you also need 51 trucks, 51 lawnmowers, 51 weed whackers, and so on. You will find that your total capital cost to build a 10-million-dollar landscape business is $1.275 million. That is a very reasonable amount, and one that you can finance using the methods we discussed in chapter 1.

As you can see, your focus should always be based on unit-level economics at the operating level. Of course, you will have additional expenses as you grow. You'll need an office, managers, people to answer the phones, computers, software, sales and marketing, payroll, and HR services. All of these SG&A expenses need to be provided for. Recall, though, that our mathematical formula already accounts for these expenses. Remember when I said we can spend up to 20 percent on those costs? My rule of thumb is gross profit (revenue minus direct operating costs) minus the minimally acceptable pretax net profit (10 percent) equals the SG&A you can spend:

$$\underbrace{\textbf{(Gross Profit}}_{\substack{\text{How Well} \\ \text{I Run The} \\ \text{Business}}} - \underbrace{\textbf{10\%)}}_{\substack{\text{Minimum} \\ \text{Profit} \\ \text{Acceptable}}} = \underbrace{\textbf{SG\&A I Can Spend}}_{\substack{\text{What I Can Spend To} \\ \text{Manage the Business}}}$$

Said another way, *how well you operate the business, minus your desired net profit, equals how much you can spend to manage the business!* Ultimately, though, if your SG&A is higher than 20 percent, you need to work on your overhead costs by attacking your sales expense, executive compensation, management layers, accounting, legal, HR, benefits, office rents, and so on. Remember, you need to build the perfect small business before you can build the perfect empire, so get these things right at this size, before you reach Stage 3.

STAGE 3: $10 MILLION TO $100 MILLION

Just as you did in the first two stages of growth, you can mathematically determine how many customers you will need to

reach $100 million in revenue. What you will almost invari-
ably find is that, to reach the required number of customers,
you will need to expand into new geographic markets.

Be strategic about what markets you move into. Let's
say, for example, that your initial MSA is Dallas/Fort Worth.
Your logical expansion markets might include Oklahoma
City, Waco, Houston, San Antonio, and Austin. That's
because, by staying within a few hours of your initial MSA,
you can easily send needed resources and support to your
new location as you work to get it off the ground.

When you start to open new offices, focus on the unit-
level economics for the new area. Your variables may be different, so you will need to refine your model, but the goal is
the same: get your economics right at the smallest possible
level, then scale from there.

Along with expanding into new MSAS, this is also the
time to start exploring two powerful tools for growth. The
first is mergers and acquisitions (M&A). You may be able
to speed up your growth by buying a strong existing business in your new MSA, then using it as your launching pad
into the new territory. And, because you got your unit-level
economics right in the first stages of growth, you will have
enough cash flow in this stage to finance your acquisition.

We will cover more on using M&A as an empire-building strategy in chapter 8.

Second, your first potential exit starts to come into play during this stage. We'll dive into exits in far greater detail in section 4, but for now, keep in mind that you can potentially sell your business to a private equity firm that will keep the lights on and let you keep running and growing your business. We'll talk more about private equity in the next chapter, but if you choose to go this route, you can use their capital to reach $100 million more quickly.

Let me give you a pro tip that will help make your journey through this stage more successful. As you expand, consider promoting one of your best employees—someone who understands your unit-level economics really well—to branch manager. Build your business in the new MSA around them, the same way you built your core business around your first truck and crew.

Having someone who can teach new employees your winning formula is key to making sure your business is successful in new locations. Yes, you successfully scaled your overall business to a new growth stage, but your new MSA is starting from zero. To scale it up to $1 million and beyond, you need to take the same steps you did when you were growing your original location to $1 million. Promoting a trusted employee who understands the "secret sauce" that got you to that all-important milestone in the first place is key. That employee is, in essence, a duplicate of *you*—or at least the you that began the original business.

Bottom line: when you think about a new branch, prioritize putting the right pieces in place to achieve rapid growth to the first million. In our landscape business example, that means lining up a lease on the new branch office and buying the trucks, mowers, and equipment necessary to outfit your first six crews. As new customers come online, start recruiting efforts to find the crews you need to service them. Of course, you must closely monitor your variables, but since you're already an expert at your business's unit-level economics, you can have some faith that revenue and growth will come rapidly in your new market.

STAGE 4: $100 MILLION TO $1 BILLION

That brings us to Stage 4: $100 million to $1 billion. The key to success at this stage might surprise you; in essence, it's all about changing gears. What do I mean by that? Simple—you need to let go of obsessively controlling every little detail.

Getting to the first $1 million (and even the first $10 million) requires you to be what I respectfully refer to as an anal-retentive control freak. This isn't a bad thing; in the beginning stages, you absolutely need to control every decision to ensure the unit-level economics are right. Somewhere around the $30 million mark, though, you're going to run out of bandwidth. It is simply impossible to manage every little detail. You might be able to fake it in Stage 3, but by the time you get to Stage 4, you have to go from being a first-chair player in every section of the orchestra to being a conductor. In other words, this is the stage at which you need to hire good people and empower them to make decisions. You must step back from managing decisions and start managing *processes*. That's the only way to free up the bandwidth you need to continue scaling.

After buying fifty-eight companies, I can say unequivocally that making this shift is crucial if you want to build an empire. Another crucial step to finding success at this stage? Strategically exiting your business (assuming you didn't take your first bite of the exit apple in the last growth stage). Remember, you're building an empire, and by at least partially exiting—but continuing as a minority shareholder—you will bring in additional shareholders whose capital you can leverage for growth. On top of that, as a minority shareholder, you will continue to get pay-days each time your company is sold (which, in the private equity world, is about every five years). My sage adage after twenty-one years as a CEO: why sell your company once, when you can sell it two, three, or more times? My personal record is five bites of the apple at the same company over a thirteen-year period!

So, there you have it. Get your unit-level economics right. Address your make-or-break issues. Scale into adjacent markets. Consider M&A. Look into exiting your business. And finally, stop being a first-chair player and become a conductor instead. *That* is how you grow a business from a startup to $1 billion in revenue. *That* is how you build an empire.

Now that you know how to maximize your potential for success at every stage of your business, it's time to dig into private equity. In the next chapter, we'll look at what private equity is, how it works, and how you can leverage it to build your empire. After that, we will begin to assemble the tools you'll need to execute on each stage of growth covered in this chapter.

KEY TAKEAWAYS

- Despite employing almost half the American workforce, many small businesses struggle to find success. To beat the odds, you need to understand the factors that contribute to long-term success.
- Taking your business from zero to $1 million is all about getting the unit-level economics right.
- To go from $1 million to $10 million, replicate the formula that took you to $1 million—and address your make-or-break issues.
- Reaching $100 million in revenue requires expanding into adjacent geographic markets.
- Before you can reach $1 billion in revenue, you must shift your mindset from "first-chair player" to conductor.

FOUR

PRIVATE EQUITY
The Empire Builder's Secret Weapon

T HROUGHOUT THIS FIRST SECTION, WE'VE FOCUSED on getting the pieces in place to lay the groundwork for your empire. We've looked at the importance of investing in what you know and creating a business that services needs over wants. We've talked about culture and becoming a magnet employer. We've also discussed what's required to succeed at each stage of your business's growth. We've covered a lot of ground—but there's one more foundational discussion we need to have before we get into the specific tools and strategies you will use to build your empire. It's time to focus on private equity (PE).

A caveat before we start: PE is an incredibly complex subject. There's no way we can cover it in depth in a single chapter, so I strongly urge you to dig deeper into the world of PE by reading my first book, *The Private Equity Playbook*, if you haven't already done so. For now, though, let's zero in on what you need to know about private equity from the standpoint of building your empire.

WHY YOU SHOULD CARE ABOUT PRIVATE EQUITY

When we talked about the stages of growth in the last chapter, it should have been abundantly clear to you that, when you're growing your company and building your empire, there will be times when you need large amounts of capital. There will also be times when you will seek to monetize your business by either partially or fully exiting. These are two crucial parts of empire building—and quite often, PE is the key to both of them.

Over the last thirty years, PE has quietly become the world's largest source of non-bank capital. When I started my career as a CEO in 2001, there were about 1,600 PE firms. Collectively, those firms had around $800 billion in assets under management (AUM). Sure, those are big numbers, but relative to the global economy, they certainly aren't awe-inspiring. Over the last several decades, though, private equity has exploded. There are now over 6,000 PE firms and more than $5 trillion in AUM, and private equity currently buys 50 percent of all companies sold worldwide.

This explosion of private equity firms means you can leverage PE to drive growth no matter what stage your business is in. In other words, when you understand how private equity works, you can use it to become more efficient, scale faster, *and* maximize your business's value when you get ready to exit.

Here's the thing, though: as important as private equity is, most entrepreneurs and business owners don't understand it. How do I know? Because over the past several years, during my seminars, speaking engagements, and guest lecturer opportunities, I've given my audiences the same ten-question multiple-choice quiz about general private equity facts. And yet, even though the people I'm quizzing are savvy business owners, millionaires, and Fortune 500 executives, 90 percent of them fail the quiz miserably. That tells me that, while most people have heard the term *private equity*, very few have even a rudimentary understanding of what it is or how it works.

If you, like so many other business owners, don't understand PE, pay close attention to this chapter. We're going to talk in some detail about what it is, how it operates, and (perhaps most importantly for our purposes) how you can leverage the PE pyramid to build your empire. Let's get started.

PRIVATE EQUITY, DEFINED

When I'm explaining PE to someone for the first time, I like to compare it to a mutual fund. Mutual funds, as you may know, aggregate money from a number of investors, and then the fund manager invests that money in various stocks. Importantly, the investors have no control over the fund manager's investment decisions. They do, however, have the ability to pull their money out at any time; mutual funds have instant liquidity.

In many ways, private equity is very similar to mutual funds. It gets capital from investors. There's a general partner (equivalent to a fund manager for this analogy) who invests that capital to buy various businesses. The investors (referred to as limited partners, or LPS) commit capital for a ten-year period. Like investors in a mutual fund, LPS have no say in what investments are made or how their capital is invested. However, *unlike* a mutual fund, there is no liquidity, it's private, and it requires a large minimum investment (usually $5 million). Private equity firms must also return their LPS' money at the end of the fund's lifecycle. During the investment period, the fund acquires companies and works to improve them. Then, in the second half of the fund's life, they will start selling the companies they purchased at auction. As they do, their LPS will receive distributions from the net proceeds of those sales.

There are various types of PE firms. Traditional firms, which include companies like Blackstone, KKR, and Apollo, raise capital from multiple people. There are also family offices, which act like traditional PE firms in terms of how they invest their capital. However, unlike traditional firms, their capital comes from a single family's wealth. Family offices include firms like MSD Capital (the family office of Michael S. Dell, the founder of Dell Computers), Rockefeller Capital Management, and Bezos Expeditions.

There are also what are referred to as captive funds. Their capital is sourced and self-invested from employees in a fixed group. Some examples of captive funds include CalPERS (California Public Employees' Retirement System), Ontario Teachers' Pension Plan, and OMERS (Ontario Municipal Employees' Retirement System). Unlike traditional firms, captive funds don't need to raise capital; they get it from the regular contributions employees make to the fund.

There are also multiple fund types. The most common is the *buyout fund*; as the name implies, this type of fund "buys out" mature companies with a strong track record of revenue and earnings. The next most common fund type is the *debt fund*. This type loans money to PE firms or other companies that need capital for investment purposes or to shore up their balance sheets (they typically loan at higher interest rates than banks would). Most people have heard of the third most common type of fund: *vc funds*. These have been made famous by TV shows like Shark Tank, but the truth of the matter is that VC is a relatively small part of the overall capital invested in PE. Unlike buyout funds, VCs generally invest in startups and ideas they think will be the next big thing. Finally, you have what are called *fund of funds*. These invest in multiple PE firms and funds at the same time, which spreads the investment risk from one firm and one fund to several firms and several funds through one investment.

So, to recap: PE firms are similar to mutual funds. The general partner makes all the investment decisions and assumes all compliance-related risks and duties. The LPS have no authority over the investments. And they send money when it's requested (up to their capital commitment) and receive distributions (net of fees) when the companies they purchased are sold.

THE PRIVATE EQUITY MONEY FLOW

Despite private equity's many similarities to mutual funds, how money flows in the world of PE is quite different. If you wanted to invest in a mutual fund, you would do so by writing a check or making a transfer upfront. When it comes to PE, though, you commit to sending capital over the ten-year lifecycle of the fund whenever the firm issues a capital call.

A capital call is when, at various points in the fund's lifecycle, a PE firm will contact its LPS to request a proportional amount of the capital required to buy a given company. If an LP is a 1 percent investor in the fund, for example, they would send the firm $100,000 in response to a $10 million capital call. One important fact to understand about private equity is that firms typically invest around 6 to 8 percent (and no more than 12 percent) of their current fund into any one company, so fund sizes dictate each firm's target investment size. Generally, capital calls are made in the first five years of the fund's life.

Throughout the book, you'll notice that I refer to the almost unlimited capital that PE can provide to empire builders like you. Let's take a moment to talk about how that capital works. No matter what size they are, PE firms buy the companies they invest in. That means if a PE firm buys your company, you get a big payday and the opportunity to become a minority investor in the company you used to own (if, as I recommend, you roll over a portion of your windfall). As the majority shareholder, the PE firm now has control, and they can borrow money from banks or invest their money directly into the company they now own to supercharge its growth. And, in the rare instances where a PE firm chooses to become a minority shareholder (rather than buying a controlling stake in the company), the capital that the firm uses to buy the minority stake is typically used for growth. In either case—thanks to their debt relationships, size, and various other factors—whether they choose to borrow from banks or invest their own money, PE firms have almost unlimited access to capital. That means if you play in the PE world, you do too.

Now that we've looked at how money flows from PE to you, let's turn our attention to something else you may be wondering about: how PE firms make money. They do this by what's known in the industry as *2 and 20*. The "2" refers to the 2 percent annual management fee PE firms charge on the capital they invest in companies. Those investment fees are typically paid for by the companies owned by the fund itself. The "20" refers to the PE practice of charging a 20 percent carried interest fee on every dollar of profit an investment makes. Put more simply, after a company is sold, 20 cents of every dollar of profit made goes to the PE firm. I think of the 2 percent annual management fee as a "keep the lights on" fee. It helps the firm pay its overhead. The 20 percent carried interest fee is how firms generate their profit and wealth.

THE PRIVATE EQUITY PYRAMID

Remember when I told you that over the past few decades, the number of PE firms and AUM have exploded? There's a reason PE has grown so rapidly—and it's not because these firms suck at investing money. Quite the opposite, in fact: private equity has, on average, more than doubled the returns offered by the S&P 500. Ultimately, despite its lack of liquidity, as long as PE outperforms the stock market, money will continue to flood into this asset class.

The incredible growth that PE has enjoyed and will continue to enjoy has big ramifications for anyone who wants to build an empire because the sheer number of PE firms means there is a firm for every size of business.

To help you wrap your head around this, think about the totality of PE firms as a pyramid. As you can see in the following illustration, the bottom of the pyramid is comprised of PE funds of less than $1 billion. Remember, firms typically only invest 6–8 percent (and no more than 12 percent) of a fund into any one company, so those with less than $1 billion must focus on companies with a relative EBITDA of $0–15 million.

As you move up the pyramid, the multiple paid for a company increases. That's because the number of companies at that larger size rapidly decreases. In the US alone, for example, there are about 33 million companies that fit into the bottom two levels of the pyramid. However, there are only 3,000 companies *on the planet* that have $1 billion in revenue. Because large companies are rare, the prices paid for them go up—and the number of firms that can afford them goes down.

THE PE PYRAMID

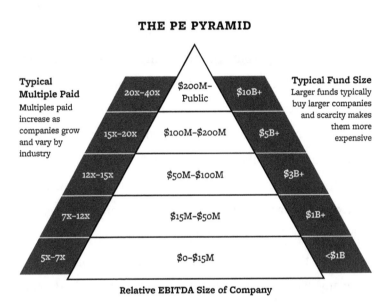

Relative EBITDA Size of Company

Remember, too, that PE firms only have ten years to execute on their fund's capital before they must give investors their money back. The larger firms simply can't buy enough companies in the bottom levels of the pyramid to effectively put their money to work. Keep this in mind as you start to leverage PE to grow your empire: small funds buy small companies, and large funds buy large companies. PE is very disciplined; as an empire builder, it behooves you to understand how this PE pyramid works, where the capital goes, and what these different value inflection points are. After all, if you understand these things, you can take the opportunity to exit at certain strategic points. Think about it. As you move up from one level of the pyramid to the next, old capital is leaving and new capital is arriving. In other words, the PE firms that take companies from $0 to $15 million EBITDA are not the same firms that will take companies from $15 million to $50 million EBITDA. As a company reaches a new value point, a smaller PE firm will sell it upstream to a larger firm. That means, if you play the game right, you can have five different private equity owners as you climb the pyramid on your way to becoming a public company. That's five different sources of capital you can use to supercharge your growth and get potentially lucrative paydays each time one firm exits and another comes in.

LEVERAGE PRIVATE EQUITY TO GENERATE WEALTH

I spent a career building wealth through private equity. I truly believe that partnering with PE firms, with their nearly unlimited capital resources and debt relationships, yields a better outcome and a higher level of income over time than maintaining 100 percent ownership of your company and trying to build an empire entirely on your own. As a business owner, your resources are limited. But when you partner with a PE firm, you get access to the resources you need as you work to build your empire. You can benefit from riding PE's coattails—as long as you understand what private equity is, how it works, and how to leverage it.

Ultimately, no matter what stage of growth your business is in, as an entrepreneur, it's crucial that you understand private equity. It's a vitally important tool to use as you build your empire and diversify your asset base.

Now that we've covered the foundational pieces of building your empire, it's time to start talking strategy. In the next section, we'll start assembling the basic tools you'll need to bend the growth curve and scale your business.

KEY TAKEAWAYS

- Despite being the world's largest source of non-bank capital and a key tool in the journey to build an empire, the vast majority of entrepreneurs, business owners, and executives don't understand private equity.

- PE is similar in many ways to mutual funds. Some key differences are that private equity requires a large minimum investment and does not offer liquidity.
- There are three main types of PE firms: traditional, family offices, and captive funds.
- There are four main types of PE funds: buyout, debt, VC, and fund of funds.
- Private equity firms issue capital calls to their limited partners over the first five years of a fund's lifecycle. In the last half of the fund's cycle, limited partners begin to receive distributions from the firm's investments as the companies are sold.
- When you understand the PE Pyramid, you can identify the right size PE firm to drive your business to the next stage of growth.

SECTION 1 WRAP-UP

There's a famous saying: *Rome wasn't built in a day.* The same holds true for building your own empire. While we will discuss the growth rate you should aim for in the next section, keep in mind that, much like you would if you were building a house, you must build your business and your empire piece by piece and step by step. This starts with focusing on building a business that serves people's needs rather than their wants. Doing so will help insulate you from economic downturns and make your business more valuable to buyers when you prepare to exit.

Whether you start from scratch or buy a pre-existing business, you must also make sure you have a strong culture and take steps to become a magnet employer in your industry so you can attract and retain the talent you'll need to successfully build and scale.

Another key foundational piece is getting your unit-level economics right. I can't emphasize this point enough: when you get things dialed in at the smallest level possible, you virtually guarantee that your business will scale successfully.

As you grow, you must also focus on implementing the other strategies (relevant to your business's size) we discussed in chapter 3: addressing your make-or-break issues, expanding into adjacent geographic markets, and learning to become a conductor instead of a first-chair player.

Finally, it's imperative that you develop a working understanding of private equity. It will be well worth your time; not only can PE provide you with almost unlimited resources to accelerate your growth, but you can also leverage private equity as you look to exit (or partially exit) at various revenue milestones.

There's one final takeaway I want to share with you before we move on to the next section: *success begins in the mind*. Learn to break down your own barriers and develop confidence in your ability to build an empire. No matter where you're starting from, recognize that you aren't yet perfect, and start taking steps *today* to learn, improve, and grow. I know—talking about getting into the right mindset can sometimes seem like nebulous advice, but that doesn't make it any less crucial to your success. Ultimately, without a mindset of success, you will struggle to implement the tools and strategies I share throughout the book.

Now that you have a solid foundation for your empire, it's time to start assembling the basic tools you can use to grow. We'll kick things off in the next chapter by talking about a four-step process you can use to bend the growth curve and transform your business.

BASIC EMPIRE-BUILDING TOOLS

To create an empire, there are several core tools and strategies you must master. I began developing these tools during my tenure at General Electric and perfected them as a CEO who specialized in turning around struggling businesses. And I continue to apply them to companies I consult for and whose boards I sit on.

While I refer to these as "basic" tools (to differentiate them from the "advanced" tools we'll discuss in section 3), they are key to supercharging your business's trajectory. I've seen this firsthand time and again: if you learn how and when to apply these basic tools, you'll be able to bend your company's growth curve and create a highly profitable, scalable business that can eventually become an empire.

Every tool and strategy I share in this section will work for any business in any industry. And here's the best part: while I first developed them to help turn around older businesses that had flatlined, they can be applied to almost any situation. You can use them to improve your startup, bend the growth curve of a mature company, or supercharge a business you've just bought. Depending on what stage your business is in or what problems it's facing, you may use one tool more heavily than another; ultimately, though, by mastering all of them, you will set yourself up for success as you build your empire.

So, let's dig in. First stop: the four-step process you can use to supercharge an existing business's growth curve.

FIVE

SUPERCHARGING YOUR GROWTH TRAJECTORY

N HIS BOOK *GOOD TO GREAT*, JIM COLLINS DESCRIBES a way to accelerate growth and put a company on a new trajectory. His advice centers around what he calls the fly-wheel effect. It's a great concept, but as an empire builder, I want you to think of it a little differently. Instead of think-ing about a flywheel, let's focus on changing your business's trajectory by *bending the growth curve.*

Before we get into how to do this, I want to make sure you're crystal clear about what sort of growth you should aim for. Remember, this section is all about assembling the basic tools you will use to supercharge your company's growth and eventually create an empire. However, the best tools in the world are useless without a solid goal to aim for, and that goal should reflect the outcome you want to achieve. In other words: set the bar for growth low, and your business won't reach its full potential. Set the bar high, and your business will rise to meet it.

SET THE RIGHT EXPECTATIONS

At this point, you might be wondering what a good bar for growth actually is. What *is* a strong annual growth rate for a company, especially a mature one? (Startups, after all, may show massive growth, but that doesn't necessarily mean they're making money. So, for the purposes of this question, let's talk about mature companies.) Whenever I teach seminars or speak at universities as a guest lecturer, I always pose the annual growth rate question to my attendees. Most of the time, the answer I get back is 10 percent. On the surface, it makes sense. Ten percent means double-digit growth! But is that enough to build an empire?

To answer that, let's consider a financial rule known as the *Rule of 72*. Essentially, this rule says that if an investment is growing at a rate of 10 percent, it will take 7.2 years to double in size. Likewise, if it's growing at 7.2 percent, it will take 10 years to double in size. Granted, the Rule of 72 is about investment returns over time, but it applies to how quickly a business can grow, too.

I want you to think about the Rule of 72 in terms of building an empire. Remember, you're taking your business through the stages of growth we talked about in chapter 3— all the way up to a billion dollars. Well, I'm going to level with you: at a 10 percent growth rate, it'll take more time than you probably have left in your working life to reach that goal. Heck, depending on what your current revenue is, getting to $1 billion may take more time than you have left on the *planet*! If your business currently does $1 million in revenue each year, it will take 7.2 years to get to $2 million. It'll take another 7.2 years to get to $4 million. It'll be *another* 7.2 years to get to $8 million. That's more than 20 years, and we aren't even at $10 million yet!

If we look at it through a private equity lens, it's no better. In a seven-year period, a 10 percent growth rate yields a 2X multiple of invested capital (MOIC). Bottom line, 10 percent just isn't good enough. In fact, it sucks. To build an empire, you need to move faster. In fact, the *minimum* acceptable annual growth rate you should aim for is 30 percent. At that rate, your company will double in size in 2.8 years. It will triple in size in 4.2 years. And, it will quadruple in size in just over five years. Those are the sort of results you need if you want to build an empire.

BENDING THE CURVE STARTS WITH DISCOVERY

Achieving a 30 percent growth rate (or better) isn't easy to do, but it's also not impossible. We'll dive into specific tools you can use to do this in the next two chapters, but for now, I want to share the four-step process I've used to consistently take mature, stagnant businesses and bend their growth curve to 30 percent or better—and sustain that growth for an extended period of time. And yes, even if your business is in the startup phase, it's worth paying attention here. No matter what stage of growth you're in, this is the process that underpins our entire empire-building toolkit.

The first step in the transformation process is discovery. Some of you may remember the TV show *House*. If so, you'll recall that Dr. House specialized in diagnosing rare and unusual infectious diseases; without fail, he would run a multitude of tests to determine what was wrong with the patient. Crucially, he didn't come in with any pre-existing notions. Instead, he cast a wide net and focused on collecting as much data as possible. In your discovery phase, aim to be like Dr. House.

When I was a CEO entering a new business for the first time, I always started with discovery. I would ask HR for a census so I knew exactly how many employees the company had and what jobs they held. I would then divide them into broad categories—for example, service technicians, salespeople, and construction workers. Then, I would get in the trenches with people from each broad category. My goal was to do a deep dive into their world. I went on ridealongs, worked alongside them to complete their tasks, and made sure they got to know me, too (remember, culture and revenue are correlated). I spent time talking to executives and customers as well.

I had no agenda; I was simply collecting data and making observations. Like Dr. House, I was casting a broad net. In every interaction, I asked tons of questions. What did they love about their job? What did they hate about it? What did they love about the company? What did they hate about it? What was hard? What was inefficient? What worked really well? And so on. Throughout the discovery phase, I observed, listened, and took copious notes. As you go through your own discovery, you need to do the same.

LOOK FOR THE UNSEEN

While you are in the discovery phase, remember that it's as important to look for the things you *don't* see as well as the things you do. There's a wonderful real-life story that illustrates this well. During WWII, the Allied forces spent considerable time analyzing battle damage to aircraft. Every time a plane returned from a combat mission, they mapped out where the bullet holes were, so they could figure out how to build a better airplane.

The dots in the image represent where returning planes had been hit by bullets. At first, the Allies wanted to reinforce the dotted areas. Eventually, though, as they considered what they *didn't* see, they realized the planes that didn't return were the ones that had taken damage in the white areas. In other words, it was the white areas, not the dotted ones, that needed to be reinforced. By considering the unseen, they were able to build better, safer aircraft.

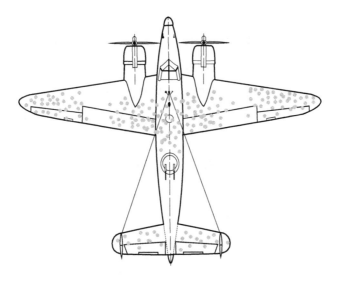

Just like the Allied forces in WWII, let go of your preconceived notions and look for what isn't immediately apparent.

DEVELOP A THESIS AND A STRATEGIC PLAN

Once you've completed discovery, it's time to develop your thesis. Remember all those notes I told you to take while you were out in the field observing and talking to people? Review them in their totality, and consider what the data is telling you. As you do, look for themes and connections.

For example, perhaps as you start to connect the dots, you realize the business's top-line revenue is stalled and its margins are steadily eroding. You may also notice there's no strategy for the future, or that the culture is strained because leadership is disconnected from employees. Create your thesis by writing down the themes you find. By doing so, you can start thinking about what initiatives you must focus on to drive growth upward.

That brings us to phase three: developing a strategic plan. We'll get into strategic plans in more detail in chapter 9, but for now, the main point I want to make is that a good strategic plan is initiative-based. That's why it's so important to collect your data and develop a thesis *before* you create your plan. There might be a thousand things wrong with the company, but by identifying the core issues through your thesis, you can identify five or six top initiatives that will move the needle forward on growth.

Remember, Rome wasn't built in a day, and you're not going to hit a 30 percent growth rate overnight. However, by defining and focusing on a handful of key initiatives, your empire will start to take shape, brick by brick and stone by stone.

MEASURE, ADJUST, REPEAT

Once you've identified your top initiatives, it's time for the final step in the transformation process: implementing your strategic plan. There are a few key things to keep in mind as you do this. First, your initiatives must be measurable. What gets measured gets done, so if a particular initiative doesn't have a measurement system in place, set it aside (or find a way to measure it so you know if it's making an impact).

Second, assign ownership and accountability for each initiative to members of your leadership team. Empower them to build teams or bring in subject matter experts to execute the initiatives. I've said it before, and I'll say it again: you have to learn to be the conductor, not a first-chair player. That means focusing on steering your team and managing the entire strategic plan, rather than taking ownership of any one initiative.

Finally, regularly review the progress being made. As you do, keep in mind that making some progress on a handful of things is better than making no progress at all. Also, remember that executing a strategic plan is an iterative process. If you don't see results, make adjustments—and keep reviewing, adjusting, and improving so you can stay on track.

As you complete initiatives and hit your goals, go back to your strategic plan, and decide what initiative you want to take on next. Remember to focus on five or six at any given time, so as one gets wrapped up, choose the next most critical one, and start focusing on it.

THE QUEST FOR $1 BILLION

When you aim for a strong growth rate and implement this four-step process, you can do amazing things. At the last company I ran as a CEO—a company that had been around for forty years, by the way—I put these steps into action. The following chart shows the annual growth rate from 2001 to 2020. Notice that before my arrival in late 2016, the average growth rate was a steady 8.9 percent. After I was hired, the growth rate increased to a steady 34 percent. This new growth trajectory allowed me to sell the company just three years later for a 4X MOIC.

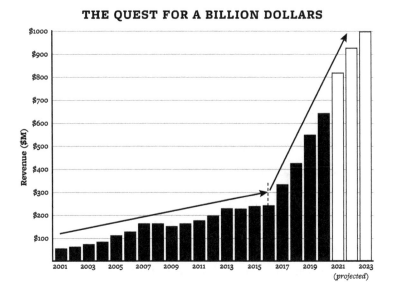

THE QUEST FOR A BILLION DOLLARS

As incredible as it is, this kind of radical upward trajectory is well within your reach, too—as long as you set the right growth expectations and get clear on how to transform your business.

Now that we've covered how to start bending the growth curve, let's get into some specific tools and strategies you can use to further boost your business's growth. In the next chapter, we're going to look at four organic growth levers you can pull to help drive your business toward a 30 percent growth rate.

KEY TAKEAWAYS

- When building your empire, aim for an annual growth rate of 30 percent or better.
- The first step to successfully bending the growth curve is to engage in discovery.
- When you're in the discovery phase, remember to look for the unseen (not just what's right in front of you).
- Once you've collected your data, use it to develop a thesis about why the business is struggling.
- Use your thesis to create an initiative-based strategic plan.
- Continually measure how your initiatives are performing; adjust if necessary to maintain forward momentum.

SIX

FOUR POWERFUL ORGANIC LEVERS

to Bend Your Growth Curve Upward

N OW THAT YOU KNOW WHAT GROWTH RATE TO
aim for, it's time to dig into the basic tools you can
use to bend your growth curve in a meaningful way
(and, just as importantly, sustain a strong upward trajectory). The first tool—and the one we'll discuss in this chapter—is increasing your business's organic growth.

There are several levers you can pull to do this. You can sell the same amount of something at a *higher* price. You can sell *more* of the same thing at the same price. You can create ancillary revenue streams or capture a new customer base. Or, you can find a way to do a combination of some or all of these.

ORGANIC GROWTH LEVER #1: PRICE

Selling your products or services for a higher price automatically yields an increase in net profit, because every penny of additional price goes right to your bottom line. That's organic growth. And here's the thing: selling your offerings for more doesn't increase your costs. In other words, price increase equals pure margin. That makes this a powerful lever to pull.

As impactful as price is, it's one of the most overlooked tools for bending the growth curve. In fact, every time I've come into a business (either as a CEO or as a consultant), I've found the same thing: nobody owns price. This is true even in large companies with thousands of employees. Over and over, it's the same story; not a single person has a full-time job dedicated to managing price. That's a problem. Maximizing this lever doesn't just magically happen; it needs to be managed. If you want to build an empire, this point is crucial to understand, so let me put it another way. Every company I've worked with—and I've worked with many—has had room to increase prices. But, because nobody is tasked with continually monitoring price, they fail to raise prices as often as they should. As a result, their growth rate suffers.

That's not the only downside that occurs when price isn't actively managed. Whether you run a product-based business or a service-based one, your costs will increase every year. If you don't raise your prices annually to compensate, you will struggle just to keep up, let alone build an empire!

I want you to go beyond merely surviving, though. I want you to thrive. So, don't simply raise prices in an attempt to offset your rising costs. Instead, prioritize the pricing lever as the powerful tool that it is by making sure that someone is actively monitoring price and using it to help drive your growth curve upward (or manage it yourself if you're running a startup or working as a solopreneur). Doing so will increase your margin and more than offset your rising costs.

Test the Waters

Don't simply guess on price. The price variable is far too important to the success of your empire. You must regularly test your pricing to see what your market will bear. Online retailers do this all the time through a process known as A/B testing. Essentially, they price the same product differently in various markets and constantly monitor what price points maximize their revenue. If you run a product-based business, you can do the same. Continually adjust your prices, and pay attention to how your sales volume is affected. Your goal is to find the sweet spot between optimal volume and optimal price.

If you have a service-based business, you can test the waters by monitoring key metrics like your close rates. In other words, compare how many quotes you put out against how many jobs you win. If your close rate is high (70 percent or more) your prices are too low. Raise them, but keep an eye on your metrics. If your close rate drops drastically (below 30 or 40 percent), lower your prices to nudge your close rates up. Keep playing with it—it's a constant balancing act because optimal price changes according to a wide variety of variables, including time of year, geographic market, and what's happening in the wider economy.

USE DATA AS A STRATEGY

In chapter 1, I mentioned the commercial laundry company I ran as a CEO (WASH Multifamily Laundry Systems). When I came in, the company had a stagnant growth rate of only 2 percent per year. With 600,000 machines in 70,000 locations, I knew every penny made a huge difference to our growth rate and bottom line. But, I also knew it was important to be smart about our pricing models. That meant using data to determine the optimal price to charge our customers.

We hired data scientists to build pricing formulas for us. They created 70,000 polynomial regression models that factored in various statistics (such as the price of gasoline, geographic area, unemployment rate, and even the day of the week) that influenced how much people would pay to do a load of laundry. Each month, we fed the latest statistical numbers into our models, which allowed us to continually refine the prices we set inside each laundromat—and drive our growth curve from 2 percent up into the double digits.

> Your business may not require 70,000 polynomial regression models, but the point remains the same. Use data to maximize your price potential and your revenue stream. If you price too high, you'll get less volume. If you price too low, you're giving up margin. Constantly experiment with price, and use data and metrics to determine what's working and what isn't.

ORGANIC GROWTH LEVER #2: VOLUME

Price is far from the only organic growth lever you should focus on. Another crucial lever is volume. Your goal should be to not only sell your offerings at a higher price but to sell *more* of your offerings at that higher price. So, as you monitor and adjust for price (either through A/B testing or by monitoring your close rate metrics), make sure you optimize for volume, too.

Along with making price adjustments, you can pump up your volume in other ways. Start with reviewing your sales strategy. How effective is your online marketing at attracting and retaining customers? Are your ad campaigns converting? What about your website? Almost every company

I've worked with has room for improvement in these areas, so take some time to audit your own strategy. You may find that redesigning your sales strategy will significantly increase your sales volume.

If your business utilizes salespeople, it may also be appropriate to hire more. If you do, be strategic about it. Consider how your core customers buy from you. Do they buy irregularly or infrequently because the products or services you offer are one-off items that last for a long time? If your company sells products or services that are "one and done," you need to hire what are known as *hunters*: salespeople who excel at acquiring new customers on an almost constant basis.

If, on the other hand, you have a lot of ancillary products or services, or your core offerings are ones that your customers buy regularly, you will be better served by hiring salespeople who are *farmers*. Just like a vegetable farmer plants seeds and then tends them to produce the greatest amount of bounty, salespeople who are farmers cultivate relationships with existing customers to get the greatest yield. They build trust with your existing customer base in order to sell them more products and services over time.

Be cognizant of which type of salesperson will best suit your needs, and hire accordingly. Remember, hunters and farmers are not cut from the same cloth. Expecting a hunter to excel at building long-term relationships is a losing proposition. So is tasking a farmer with getting out and knocking on doors to bring in new customers. Unfortunately, far too many companies don't seem to realize this—and they end up leaving both volume *and* price on the table as a result. Don't overlook the value of using both hunters and farmers in concert to maximize potential. I once ran a company that had hunters searching for new clients; after the first year, they handed them off to farmers to cultivate the relationships while they returned to knocking on new doors.

ORGANIC GROWTH LEVER #3: PIVOTING

There is another lever that is fundamental to bending the growth curve to 30 percent and beyond: pivoting. We touched on this concept when we talked about moving through the stages of growth, but it's worth exploring further here.

Once your core product or service is selling well, it's time to begin strategically pivoting. Often, this means adding ancillary products or services. Think back to the example of the landscape maintenance business in chapter 3.

The core service was mowing lawns; sprinkler repair, bed mulching, and landscape lighting are examples of strategic pivots that created new revenue streams from your existing customers. Ultimately, adding ancillary services will bend the growth curve far more quickly than if you focus exclusively on adding new products or services that require completely new customers. After all, the hard part is usually getting the customer. Once you have them, prioritize cross-sells and upsells.

We see the most successful companies doing this all the time. Think about McDonald's, for example. When someone pulls up to the drive-through and orders a Big Mac, what's the first question the cashier asks? *Would you like fries with that? And then: How about a drink? Would you like to supersize your meal? Would you like an apple pie as well?* Take a page out of their book—as you work to bend your growth curve upward, be on the lookout for more products and services you can upsell or cross-sell.

Pivoting is also extremely useful if you are in a highly competitive industry—what we refer to as a red ocean[2]

---

2   W. Chan Kim and Renée A. Mauborgne, *Blue Ocean Strategy, Expanded Edition: How to Create Uncontested Market Space and Make the Competition Irrelevant* (Massachusetts: Harvard Business Review Press, 2014).

(when the "ocean" you're swimming in is red from the blood of competitors chewing on each other, trying to win a customer). When you're stuck in a red ocean, find a way to pivot to a blue ocean instead. Let me give you an example. In 2016, I became the CEO of CoolSys, a large company that provided refrigeration services to grocery stores. However, grocery stores have notoriously low margins, which means their purchasing decisions are highly price-driven. As a result, there's intense competition for their business—a textbook case of a red ocean.

When I came in, I realized this was keeping our growth rate and margins depressed. So, I focused on finding ways to strategically pivot to blue oceans. I didn't drop our core customers, of course, but I did create two new divisions by buying several engineering and HVAC service companies to increase our core offerings. Then, I used those acquisitions to start offering engineering, HVAC, and refrigeration services to blood banks, telecommunication customers, data centers, and pharmaceutical storage facilities.

Bottom line: when your margins are getting bloodied by your competition, find blue ocean markets where customers will pay more and the competition is less fierce. That will allow you to charge a higher price and earn a higher margin (we will talk about other ways to enhance margin in the next chapter).

> The CoolSys example brings up an important point. The companies I acquired were all in adjacent customer segments, but unlike grocery stores, they weren't primarily focused on price. Instead, they prioritized quality and speed of service delivery. By acquiring these companies, we were able to offer our customers those value-adds, which meant we were able to sell more services for a higher price. In turn, that boosted our growth and improved margins. As you are building your empire, look for opportunities to do the same.

ORGANIC GROWTH LEVER #4:
TIERING PRODUCTS AND SERVICES

There's one more organic growth lever every empire builder should have in their toolkit: tiering products and services. Whether you sell products or services, tiering will increase your total addressable market (TAM) and create new price points, which will pull both the volume *and* the price levers.

A great example of a product-based company that has mastered tiering is Mercedes-Benz. Their flagship car is called the S-class. I don't know what the S stands for, other than 'spensive—it retails for upward of $100,000. As nice as the S-class is, there are people out there who want the cachet of driving a Mercedes but don't have six figures to spend on a car. Mercedes-Benz understands that, so they created the E-class. (Know what the E stands for, at least in my mind? *Economy.* Instead of spending $100,000, you can get an E-class for around $60,000.) And then, they went a step further. They created the C-class for people who value their brand but can't afford $60,000 for a car. The C, of course, stands for *cheap.* I'm being flippant here, but you get the point. By tiering its product and creating three subsets within its larger core offering, Mercedes-Benz increases its TAM, which in turn, increases its volume and its profit. If you have a product-based company, you can do the same.

Tiering is also incredibly effective for service-based businesses. A great example is FedEx. They offer a variety of delivery services; the faster the delivery, the more the service costs. Just like Mercedes, tiering in this way allows

FedEx to increase its TAM. They can service customers who need fast delivery and are willing to pay a premium for it (which pulls FedEx's price lever), but they remain competitive among customers who are looking for economical options (which maintains volume).

One note about tiering: always do it in threes. Data shows that the largest segment of your customer population—somewhere around 60 percent—will buy the middle-tier product or service. Anywhere from 10 to 20 percent will gravitate to your premium offering. The remaining percentage will buy your least expensive product or service. If you want to create subsets within those three tiers, you can, as long as you do that in threes, too.

IT'S TIME TO START PULLING THE LEVERS

There you have it: some proven strategies to drive up growth. Now, I want you to think about your own business. What is your current growth rate? To build an empire, you need to get it upward of 30 percent, so take a look at your business and determine which of these concepts you need to apply to start bending the curve.

Remember, it's imperative to assign someone in your organization to own (and continually monitor) price. Test the waters, too, to optimize price and volume. Metrics are key, after all, and as an empire builder, you should be using data to monitor and refine your organic growth strategies. At the same time, consider updating your sales strategy by revamping your web presence, improving your ads, and adding hunters and/or farmers to your salesforce. Finally, consider the many ways you can strategically pivot (especially if you're swimming in a red ocean), and find ways to tier your products and services.

Taking all of these actions will help you put your growth on a strong upward trajectory and prepare you for the next step: enhancing your margins. We'll dig into how to do that in the next chapter.

KEY TAKEAWAYS

- To bend your growth curve upward, focus on selling more of your offerings at a higher price.

- Assign someone in your organization to continually monitor and adjust price, and make sure they test the waters to optimize price and volume.
- Redesign your sales strategy to pump up your volume.
- Strategically pivot by adding ancillary products and services and expanding into adjacent customer segments.
- Tier your products and services to pull multiple organic growth levers.

SEVEN

MAKE YOUR TOP AND BOTTOM LINES SOAR

HERE'S NO DOUBT THAT ORGANIC GROWTH LEVERS are foundational to building your empire. Used correctly, they can significantly increase your top line and supercharge your growth curve. But there's another basic tool every empire builder needs in their toolkit as they work to reach a CAGR of 30 percent (or better). That tool is margin enhancement.

There are multiple strategies—five, in fact—you can use to boost your margin and pass more revenue to your bottom line. In this chapter, we'll look at how you can apply each of them in your business as you grow your empire.

IT STARTS WITH MINDSET

Before we get into the specific strategies of margin enhancement, I want to talk for a moment about why this particular tool is so important. Essentially, it comes down to cost pressures. In chapter 6, we touched on the fact that the costs to run your business will go up every year. Inflation is a fact of life, and if your prices don't increase correspondingly, you'll struggle to break even, let alone make a strong profit.

According to statistics from the World Bank, in 2020, the US inflation rate was 1.23 percent. In 2021, that rate increased to 4.70 percent, and in 2022, it jumped to a whopping 8 percent. (Inflation, by the way, affects a wide variety of things: wage creep, rising healthcare costs, increases in fuel prices, higher material costs, and so on.) This kind of cost pressure has the potential to seriously reduce your profitability as you work to build your empire.

To counteract this, you must have a mindset of continuous improvement. In other words, you must continually refine your operations to offset inflationary pressures and increase your bottom line. That's exactly what the strategies we're going to discuss in this chapter will help you do.

CREATE OPERATING LEVERAGE

One of the best ways to enhance margin is to take advantage of what's known as *operating leverage* (first discussed in chapter 3). For this strategy to work, you must be operating at some scale. However—and this is important—even if you're too small to utilize it right now, once you understand how operating leverage works, you'll be prepared to use it when you're big enough.

If you recall, in the fictional landscape business we introduced in chapter 3, we determined you needed 6 trucks (with 6 crews) to hit $1 million. To reach $10 million, you needed 51 crews and 51 trucks. Thanks to the power of volume discounts, buying 6 trucks will get you a better price than buying just one, and buying 51 trucks will get you a larger discount than buying 6.

That's operating leverage in action. As you get bigger, your purchasing volume increases. You can capitalize on that to pass more of your revenue through to the bottom line. And you know what? When you combine a strong bottom line with an increase in your top-line growth, *you have the makings of an empire.*

TECHNOLOGY IS KEY

As helpful as operating leverage is, it's far from the only way to enhance margin. Another key strategy is to unlock human productivity by investing in technology.

Take WASH Multifamily Laundry Systems, the laundry service company I told you about in chapter 1, for example. On any given day, we had hundreds of service technicians who would drive to customer locations to repair broken equipment. Once they arrived, they inspected the customer's equipment, diagnosed the problem, and then repaired it. Sometimes, they needed a specific part they didn't have on their truck. In those instances, they had to drive to a different location to get the part, then return to the customer's location to complete the repair.

Every time our technicians engaged in low-value work (driving to a customer's site or driving somewhere to pick up a part), they drove down our profitability and decreased our margins. And since we had hundreds of technicians, this was happening at scale. The solution? Use technology to automate their low-value work so they could spend more of their time doing high-value work (i.e., making repairs).

Given the vast amount of technology available, there are multiple ways to do that. Imagine this scenario (which plays out for businesses around the world every single day): a technician gets up in the morning and checks their smartphone or handheld device. They can immediately see where their first call is because of technology that parses service call requests out to them based on the customer's geographic location and the volume of calls coming in. At the same time, the technology prepares an optimized route for them to get to each call, which reduces drive time and fuel expenditures and maximizes the number of customer calls they can do in a day.

Because each technician's truck has vehicle-tracking technology, they are automatically clocked in as soon as they leave home to go to the first service call. They don't have to waste time on low-value work like filling out a time card or calling into an interactive voice response (IVR) system. When they arrive at their customer's location, another piece of technology automatically opens a service ticket and, if appropriate, starts charging the customer for labor. If the customer needs to be notified that the technician is on-site, an email or text message is automatically sent.

Utilizing technology in this way streamlines the technician's workload. But, it can do even more. Based on multiple service incidents, a database that utilizes machine learning predicts what parts the technician will need to fix the equipment. It sends the tech a message specifying what part they will likely need *and* tells them exactly where the part is located in their truck. That way, the technician doesn't have to waste time searching for the part or driving somewhere else to get it; they can simply walk in with the part in their hand. Furthermore, when the technician pulls the part off the truck, they scan a barcode on it with their device. At that point, the customer is automatically billed for the item (if appropriate), and the inventory system is automatically updated so more parts can be ordered.

Thanks to technology, the technician hasn't spent time talking to anyone, ordering parts, making unnecessary trips, or filling out paperwork. The majority of their time has been spent doing high-value work—and the same story will play out for the next customer, and the next, and the next, resulting in a dramatic increase in margin and productivity.

ADD TRUE VALUE TO YOUR BUSINESS

Maximizing high-value work and minimizing low-value work can be done for almost any job. Take your Accounts Payable/Accounts Receivable (AP/AR) people, for example. They may have hundreds of tasks they must accomplish every month. Some of these may be high-value tasks, and some may be low-value. Once again, you can streamline their processes.

Let's say, for example, they are doing repetitive data entry hundreds of times in a given month. Can you find technology that will accomplish that task for them? If not, can you outsource that task (which they probably hate doing anyway)?

Automation (or outsourcing) is not about getting rid of employees. It's about maximizing their productivity by enabling them to spend as much time as possible on high-value work. The key is to define each of your employee groups' low-value and high-value work. Then, think about how to automate or outsource the low-value tasks (and the tasks they despise doing) so they can focus on things that add real value to your operation.

CHALLENGE THE STATUS QUO

Admiral Grace Hopper once said, "The most dangerous phrase in the English language is, 'We've always done it this way.'" She was absolutely right. As you're building your empire, it's not enough to just implement technology or utilize operating leverage. You must also be willing to challenge the status quo. A great example of how powerful it is to challenge convention comes from the laundry company I ran, WASH Multifamily Laundry Systems.

Remember in chapter 5 when we talked about the importance of the discovery phase? Well, when I came on as CEO of WASH Multifamily Laundry Systems in 2003, part of my discovery included going on ride-alongs with the employees (*collectors*) who collected the quarters from the laundry machines. This was before the widespread use of electronic payment systems in laundry rooms. It quickly became apparent that there was a complex set of security measures collectors had to go through to get the coins out of each machine. The process, which had been in place for decades, was overly complicated. Among other measures, each machine had its own key, which meant each collector had to carry about 500 keys per day on a key string. And each day, the collectors needed a different key string for the machines they would visit as part of their normal collection route.

I started asking why. Why did every machine have its own key? Why were there security guards literally watching the keys to the machines in every office around the country? Why were we making it so hard for our employees to collect the quarters? I asked a lot of people, but nobody could give me any answers.

Finally, I came across an employee who had worked at the company for more than forty years. He told me that back in the early 1960s, there was a huge problem with "gentleman lockpicks." These people (who dressed nicely to avoid attracting attention) would go into the laundromat, pick the locks on the machines, steal the quarters, then put the machines back together so the company was less likely to notice the theft. To defeat this widespread issue, the company implemented various complex measures—including a different key for each one of their thousands of machines. The security measures the company put in place were so effective that the "gentleman lockpicks" completely ceased to be a problem, but the processes were never updated to reflect that.

I was determined to change things. Armed with the information I learned in discovery, my catchphrase became "One room, one key, one lock." In other words, the same key would now open up every machine in the room. That meant that instead of 500 keys per day, each collector could carry just 100.

Because they no longer had to shuffle through hundreds of keys to find the exact key that would fit one particular machine, each collector's productivity increased by over 40 percent. (In fact, they were able to collect so many more coins that we ended up with a new problem: our trucks' axles were breaking under the weight of the quarters. We had to redesign them to keep up with the increase in quarters collected.) The resultant increase in earnings was measured in millions of dollars, and it was all the result of challenging the status quo.

I hope this story illustrates the fact that streamlining is about far more than simply looking at your numbers and deciding you need to cut costs by some arbitrary percentage. Let's say, for the sake of example, that you decide you want to cut your costs by 10 percent. You look at a ten-person department and decide to let one person go. Sure, you cut costs—but you didn't change the process or what that department does. Now, the nine people who are left have to pick up the slack, which can drive down morale and engagement. Remember way back in chapter 2 when we talked about how culture and revenue are directly correlated? When morale drops because of this kind of arbitrary cost-cutting measure, it can destroy your culture—and that can lead to a death spiral. A far better approach to cutting costs is to challenge convention and change thinking—and as the gentleman-lockpick story shows, it all starts with asking why.

RETHINK YOUR STRUCTURE

By challenging the status quo, automating low-value tasks, and outsourcing low-value work that can't be easily automated, you can lower your cost structures significantly. However, there's another strategy that, when implemented alongside the first three, will make a big impact on margin enhancement: rethinking structure.

I first learned this particular strategy during my time at GE. Despite having 340,000 employees, GE's goal was to make sure there were never more than five layers of management between the CEO and any given employee.

Many times, when I come into a business—small or large, startup or mature—there are far more than five layers between employees and the top leader. That increases bloat and decreases productivity and efficiency. To avoid this, make it your aspirational goal to have a flat vertical structure with no more than five layers, and a 30:1 ratio of employees to managers; in other words, every full-time dedicated manager should have thirty employees under them.

I often see a ratio of 8:1 in small businesses I consult for. As your company grows, that ratio will end up costing you more money without adding any meaningful ROI. So, challenge the status quo here, too. Look for opportunities to combine work groups, and reduce the number of dedicated managers you have. Use working supervisors or group leads to help with managing the employee efforts. Push decision-making authority as low into your organization as possible, empower those managers, and use metrics to hold them accountable. If you do, you will quickly find that because the people close to your customers are making decisions, your company's health *and* bottom line will be stronger.

PRIORITIZE WORKING ON THE BUSINESS

There's one final margin enhancement strategy I want to share with you. As you grow, focus on building a team of people whose sole responsibility is improving your business's operations.

If you run a manufacturing business, the team might be comprised of people with Six Sigma backgrounds. If you have a service-based business, you may want to bring in people with Lean Sigma experience. In all cases, though, find people who are specialists at looking at processes and procedures and finding bottlenecks and fixing them, so your operations become more streamlined and effective. This is crucial for ongoing margin enhancement.

If you're a solopreneur or still in the first stage of growth, you may find it challenging to hire a team of people to help you with process improvement. In that case, you can join a peer group and learn best practices from other people with similar businesses. This will help you build your empire more quickly and ensure your decisions have the greatest impact possible. You can also hire a knowledgeable consultant to help you redesign your processes to better drive top-line growth and increase your bottom line.

SUPERCHARGE YOUR BUSINESS INTO AN EMPIRE

Ultimately, successfully enhancing your margins starts with your mindset. You must commit to continuous improvement in your business; otherwise, it will stagnate and your bottom line will suffer.

Once you have the right mindset, though, things become much easier. As you grow, you can utilize operating leverage. You can implement technology or outsource work to minimize time spent on low-value tasks. You can challenge the status quo, rethink your structure, and bring in experts to help you fix bottlenecks and inefficiencies. By doing all of these things—*and* implementing the strategies we discussed in chapter 6—both your top and bottom lines will soar.

Now that we've covered the basic tools you'll use to build your empire, it's time to turn our attention to more advanced tools. In the next chapter, we'll look at using M&A to supercharge your business's growth into an empire.

KEY TAKEAWAYS

- Maintaining a mindset of continuous improvement is foundational for counteracting cost pressures.

- As your business grows, utilize operating leverage to pass more of your revenue through to your bottom line.
- Invest in technology to automate your workforce's low-value tasks and drive their productivity up.
- Challenge the status quo by asking why.
- Push decision-making authority as low into your organization as possible.
- Hire people (or work with a peer group or consultant) to work on your business, not in your business.

SECTION 2 WRAP-UP

After twenty-one years as a CEO running three differ-ent companies in three different industries for nine dif-ferent private equity sponsors (not to mention billions of dollars in exits), I know exactly how to build an empire. As we discussed in section 1, you need to get the foun-dational pieces right first. Once you've done that—built the right culture, created a business that focuses on needs, gotten clear on the stages of growth, and edu-cated yourself about private equity—it's time to start assembling the tools you'll use to build your empire.

The first objective is bending your business's growth curve upward to 30 percent CAGR or more. To reach that goal, you need to master the first basic tool: focusing on organic growth. To do that, increase prices, increase sales volume, strategically pivot, and tier products or services. Taking the steps necessary to pull all of these levers will have the maximum impact on your top-line revenue growth.

It's not enough to simply get more revenue, though. You've got to *keep* the revenue you earn. The best way to do that? Margin enhancement. This is the second basic tool you can implement to build your empire. Again, there are multiple strategies you can use to increase your bottom line: utilizing operating leverage, implementing technology, asking why, rethinking your structure, and bringing in experts to help you redesign your processes. I recommend you employ all of them.

Mastering these basic tools is fundamental to successfully growing your business into a billion-dollar empire. Combined with the advanced tools we'll discuss in the next section, they're what will allow you to *double* your business in 2.8 years, *triple* it in 4.2 years, and *quadruple* it in 5 years.

Remember, we only have a finite amount of time on this planet. If you want to build an empire, you must move with a sense of urgency. So, with that in mind, let's press on to the next section: mastering the advanced tools of empire building. The first tool we'll look at is M&A. See you there.

ADVANCED EMPIRE-BUILDING TOOLS

At this point, your empire-building journey is well underway. You have a solid foundation: a strong culture, the right unit-level economics, and a business that serves people's needs. You also have the basic tools to take your business—whether it's one you've started from scratch, acquired, or inherited—through the first few stages of growth. Now, it's time to talk about the advanced tools that will turn your business into a true empire.

I've talked about the importance of mindset before, but getting into the right headspace is especially critical now. Taking your business from somewhere around $100 million up to $1 billion and beyond—which is the stage we're at now—requires you to fully step into the role of conductor. That means hiring great people and empowering them to make decisions while you manage the processes. Just as importantly, it means actively considering bringing on a partner with a significant amount of capital resources and debt relationships who can supercharge your company's growth. In other words, you need to think about selling your business and making the move from majority shareholder to a minority one.

This is so important, in fact, that I will start this section with that lesson. Then, once we've talked about M&A, we'll dig into how to use strategy and management systems to achieve your business's maximum potential.

A note before we dive in: even if your business is still too small to utilize these tools in the ways we discuss, don't skip this section! There's no reason why you can't implement these advanced tools on a smaller scale. No matter what stage of growth you're in, the important thing is that you understand these advanced tools and start applying them to your business to the maximum extent possible so you can more quickly boost your growth.

Ready? Okay, let's get to it.

EIGHT

USING MERGERS AND ACQUISITIONS
to Create an Empire

B Y NOW, YOU SHOULD BE LASER-FOCUSED ON ONE goal: bending your business's growth curve to 30 percent CAGR or more. To do that, you should be pulling organic growth levers (like volume, price, pivots, and tiering) and taking concrete steps to enhance your margins.

I'm going to level with you, though: even with diligent application, very few mature companies can get to a 30 percent CAGR and hold it for an extended period of time using only the strategies we covered in the last section. Luckily, though, there is another tool that larger companies can utilize to boost and maintain growth. That tool is M&A. Also known as buy-and-build, this is the process of buying companies and putting them together to form an entity greater than the sum of its parts.

Buy-and-build is the core strategy I've used for every empire I've ever built. One of my empires, for example, was a combination of thirty-four companies. Another was a combination of twenty-three. There's a simple reason for this: buy-and-build truly is the key to creating and maintaining explosive growth in a mature company. That's because it gives you a way to acquire similar companies (or those that will support your strategic objectives in some way) in order to expand your offerings, reach, and/or customer base, and to do so quickly. Indeed, buy-and-build is how the juggernaut that is private equity achieves such incredible returns and adds the vast majority of shareholder value. And now, you're going to learn how to use this tool to achieve your empire-building dreams.

DEFINING BUY-AND-BUILD

At its core, buy-and-build is the art of acquiring a number of companies and combining them to boost value and achieve a specific goal. M&A is the fastest way to scale because it allows you to fill gaps and tap into markets you might not be able to access quickly otherwise. It's also incredibly efficient from a capital perspective because your primary source of funding is other people's money, or OPM. And, as we discussed in chapter 4, if you partner with private equity, you can tap the large streams of capital and lending capacity they have at their disposal, which makes M&A even more capital-efficient. To sum up, then, buy-and-build is a strategy that allows you to build a much larger business in a much shorter amount of time and for much less equity. Perfect for empire building, don't you think?

As great as it is, there are a few requisites for a successful M&A strategy. First and foremost, you need a fragmented industry. Remember when we talked about the phonebook test in chapter 1? That test applies here, too. For buy-and-build to work, you need an industry where there are so many companies that they can't possibly all be bought by a small handful of buyers. That's key to keeping the prices of those businesses low. Remember, a fragmented industry is akin to a buyer's market and a non-fragmented industry is akin to a seller's market. In this instance, you're the buyer, so you want fragmented industries.

Another requisite for success: when you're getting ready to embark on a buy-and-build journey, make sure you understand what a "good" acquisition looks like. Otherwise, it's far too easy to fall victim to what I call the *Shiny Penny Syndrome*, where every business you see looks perfect, and you completely miss its flaws. Of course, what constitutes "good" varies depending on your needs and goals, so it may be more accurate to say that you should have a specific profile of what you're looking for in a business before you start shopping around. If a company doesn't fit your target profile, keep looking. Don't get attached, don't fool yourself into thinking you can fix it, and don't waste your time and money trying to figure out how to make it work. Just move on. I'm speaking from personal experience here; bad acquisitions can zap your energy and resources and set you back on your empire-building journey. One real-life example: I fell victim to Shiny Penny Syndrome and bought a business that didn't fit my specific profile. It ended up causing 80 percent of my management headaches for three full years, and to make things worse, it brought in less than 5 percent of my revenue. So, heed my warning, and make sure you know what good looks like for *you* before you start looking.

The other requisite for a successful buy-and-build is to be strategic about what you're trying to achieve. Do you want to extend your current business's geographic reach quickly and efficiently? Build density in your target markets? Enable pivots by tapping into businesses that offer products or services adjacent to yours? Getting clear on your strategy will help you stay focused and avoid Shiny Penny Syndrome.

IT'S ALL ABOUT ARBITRAGE

Now that you have a sense of what it takes to make M&A successful, let's talk about how you can use this strategy to reap multiple arbitrage. If you aren't familiar with what "reaping multiple arbitrage" means, don't worry. We're going to unpack it because it's a vital concept for all empire builders to understand.

Remember our PE pyramid from chapter 4? Take a look at it again on the following page. You'll notice that as the relative EBITDA size of a company increases, the typical multiple paid increases exponentially. When you take advantage of this by buying a lot of relatively inexpensive companies (thank you, fragmented industry!) and putting them together to increase your business's size and boost its multiple, your arbitrage—which is simply the difference between the sale price of your now-bigger company and the buy price of the smaller companies—soars. In other words, you "reap multiple arbitrage."

THE PE PYRAMID

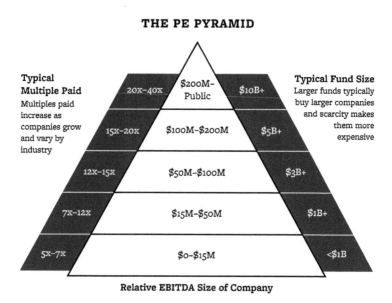

Relative EBITDA Size of Company

Let's make this concept more concrete using an example from my own career of a company I was building (for the purposes of this example, I'm going to extract and isolate just the M&A component). I started with a base platform company that the PE firm bought using a combination of equity from their fund and debt borrowed from banks. I then bought 8 companies during the first hold period with one PE group and 15 more in the second hold period with a second group. The average price paid for each acquisition was 5x EBITDA. Each of those companies averaged $2 million in EBITDA, and my borrowing (or leverage) capacity—in other words, what banks would lend me—was 5x EBITDA. Because I bought 23 companies in total with $2 million in EBITDA each, I added $46 million in EBITDA.

23 (number of companies bought) x **$2m EBITDA** (their average size) = **$46m EBITDA** (purchased).

$46m EBITDA (purchased as individual companies) was bought for **5x** (small multiple reflecting the individual value of the 23 individual components) or a total of **$230M**.

After putting the 23 companies together, we had climbed the PE Pyramid. The small companies that were individually worth 5x now comprised a larger company; the value they sold for collectively was 13x. In other words, following integration, they were no longer 23 small companies but one larger company. As discussed earlier, larger is rare—and worth more money than the smaller companies individually. When taken to market the larger company sold for 13x EBITDA because we climbed the pyramid and were rewarded with a higher valuation by the universe of buyers. That created $598 million of enterprise value for shareholders.

13x (higher valuation) x **$46m EBITDA = $598M** (the new value of the combined companies purchased).

It cost $230 million to buy these 23 companies ($46 million x 5), but the banks loaned me that money (because of my 5x leverage capacity). Yes, you read that right: I financed 100 percent of the purchase price using debt to buy these companies, which meant that the various shareholders earned $368 million in profit *with $0 of additional equity invested.*

$598M (new value) - **$230M** (the cost to buy the individual smaller, less valuable companies) = **$368M**

profit or "arbitrage" (the difference between what
I sold them for collectively versus buying them
individually).

That is the power of M&A and reaping multiple arbitrage.
As you buy smaller companies, you collect their earnings.
You integrate them together. You climb the PE pyramid,
and then you sell for a higher multiple.

Sure, you need a big checkbook to make this work, but
that's what PE brings to the table. You can leverage their
capital, and more importantly, their debt relationships. In
reality, once a PE firm buys a company, they try hard not
to put more capital in it (so they can buy additional companies with the money left in the fund). Your access to
capital benefit is primarily through relationships they have
with lenders (banks and debt funds) that get you outsized
access to large loans that a company could not get on its
own. So, access to capital through PE includes both equity
and debt. All you have to do is go out and find the companies, and you will be able to massively accelerate your
growth toward your billion-dollar empire. And, remember,
if you don't want to bring in outside capital, you can do this
yourself on a smaller scale—you'll just have to buy fewer

companies, get creative on financing, and take a bit longer to make your acquisitions.

THE STAGES OF M&A

Now that you understand the power of this tool, let's talk about how to implement buy-and-build. As the graphic below shows, the main stages of M&A include sourcing, outreach, filter, IOI–LOI, diligence, contracts, funding, closing, and integration:

BUY AND BUILD PROCESS OVERVIEW

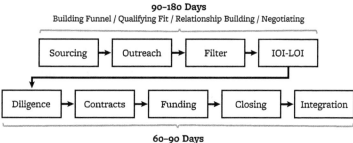

(*Note: covering M&A fully is beyond the scope of this book, which is why I highly recommend reading—or re-reading—The Private Equity Playbook before you start utilizing buy-and-build in earnest.*)

#1: Sourcing

The first step in M&A is sourcing. Essentially, sourcing means finding every company that fits the profile of target companies that you previously created—companies within your target industry and target geography. That's it. You're not filtering the companies you find. You aren't considering whether you want to buy them. You (or the buy-side advisor you outsource this task to) are simply making a list of all the companies that are in your industry within a given geography. In this step, you are loading up the funnel.

#2: Outreach

Once you've sourced potential companies, you need to figure out whether or not there are any companies that may be prospective purchases. You also need to determine if the owners of any of those companies are interested in potentially selling. If sourcing is about loading up your funnel, outreach is the first step in sorting them. Outreach can be done by a buy-side advisor, your business development team, or both.

#3: Filter

The filtering stage is focused on deciding whether or not the companies you've identified meet your target criteria (remember, having a profile is the best way to avoid the Shiny Penny Syndrome I warned you about earlier!). This, in my opinion, is the most important stage in the entire buy-and-build process. You need to be very disciplined in filtering out the bad companies so you can stay laser-focused on the good. To do that, ask questions about each company in your funnel:

- Is it the right size?
- Does it have a good reputation?
- Is it servicing the customers I am targeting?
- What are its revenues and EBITDA?
- Is it in the right industry verticals?
- And so on.

Depending on what your goals are, your list may have more than a thousand companies in it. Outreach and filtering will bring you down to the 100 or so you might be most interested in buying. Not all of them will have owners who want to exit, though, so your actual *active* target list will probably consist of ten to twenty companies at any given time.

#4: IOI–LOI

Once you've completed the filtering process, signed an NDA with an active target, and gotten some basic financial information in return, it's time to move to the next step: giving your prospective target an indication of interest (IOI) or letter of intent (LOI). These essentially say, "I like your company, and I'm interested in buying it, based on these specific terms. Based on your revenue and earnings, I'll offer you $x." If the business's owner is interested in selling, you will each sign the LOI or IOI. Both LOIS and IOIS are non-binding, but they do give you exclusivity. That's important because up to this point, you haven't spent much money on this process. However, as soon as you move to the next step, that's going to change.

#5: Diligence

In the first four steps, you didn't do much more than superficial digging into the companies you're interested in. Yes, you talked with your target company's leaders about their financials, but you took everything they said at face value and gave them a price based on that. In this step, though, all that changes. This is the point where you verify everything they've told you. That means doing a quality of earnings (Q of

E) analysis. It means bringing in accountants to review their books and accounting practices. Most of all, it means making sure the EBITDA they communicated to you is accurate.

Fair warning: if a deal is going to go south, this is the stage where it generally happens. Diligence often reveals fuzzy accounting practices or incorrect EBITDA, which obviously impacts the purchase price. It requires an enormous amount of work to make sure that what you *think* you're buying matches what you're actually buying.

Once you get through financial diligence, this stage isn't over, either—you have to move on to other diligence. Do they have good hiring practices? Is their paperwork right? Are their software and infrastructure in order? Most of this work is done by outsourced providers that specialize in each of these areas, but even still, for the seller, this step can feel like a proctology exam that never ends.

#6: Contracts

Once you get through the financial part of diligence, if everything looks good, it's time for the lawyers to write up the contracts as the rest of the diligence process continues. I can't emphasize enough how important it is to hire competent counsel for this step. You wouldn't hire your dentist to do brain surgery, and you shouldn't have any-one but lawyers experienced in M&A negotiate and draw up your contracts.

#7: Funding

The next step is to secure funding. We discussed several sources of capital in chapter 1, but to quickly recap, you can use seller financing (where the seller holds back a por-tion of the proceeds as a loan earning a market interest rate), and seller equity (where the seller becomes a roll-over minority investor, buying stock in your company). You can borrow money from the SBA or from banks. You can use self-generated cash (equity) or utilize cashless mergers (this approach is becoming increasingly popular as interest rates tick up). And, of course, if you're work-ing with private equity, you can use their capital or debt providers.

Before you even start sourcing, make sure you have the funding to buy a company. The last thing you want to do is spend time finding companies, sorting them, and filtering them, only to discover you don't have the capital to acquire them. Just like getting pre-approved to buy a house, you can get pre-funded before you begin sourcing. Whether or not you choose to do so, make sure you have an idea of where your funding will come from before you get to this stage. Trust me on this one; it will save you lots of time and stress.

#8: Closing

Once all the paperwork is complete and you've received funding, the sale can close. At this point, it's time for the final M&A stage: integration.

#9: Integration

Integration might involve the harnessing of synergies; if both companies have HR departments, for example, you may combine them into one. Integration doesn't necessarily mean firing people, but it does mean you may reallocate them to different roles.

There's no right or wrong answer when it comes to whether you should do a full or partial integration, either. It generally comes down to what the industry practice is and—more importantly—whether or not you can fully integrate or if you have an operational need that requires a partial integration. Because this step is so complex, I encourage you to hire an integration manager to help optimize the process if buy-and-build is going to be a continuous part of your growth story.

Keep in mind that if you are using buy-and-build as an ongoing strategy, you will eventually want to build an M&A team in-house. The first step to doing that is hiring someone to lead the buy-and-build effort. They should have a background as a CPA and have worked for a large regional or national accounting firm doing transactional diligence (which is essentially helping people buy and sell companies). Additionally, they should have already successfully worked on multiple deals and have a keen understanding of every step of the process. With their help, you can build your M&A team. However, at least at first, it's fine to outsource the buy-and-build process.

CONVINCING FOUNDERS TO SELL

At this point, if you're like many of the founders and entrepreneurs I talk to, you understand the value of M&A. But, you probably have a question swirling around in your head: *How can I convince someone to sell their business to me?*

I think the best approach is to frame the benefits of selling in a way that the founder or entrepreneur whose business you want to buy can understand. Help them see that selling is an exercise in asset diversification, not an exercise in selling their business and walking away. For example, you can tell them about the power of rollover investing. Rollover investing is a strategy where a seller takes some chips off the table but rolls a portion of their proceeds forward as a minority shareholder in order to get a second payday the next time the company is sold. Here is a sample formula for how this might look: for every dollar of profit the seller gets from the sale of their business, they can take 70 cents home and roll 30 cents forward. If, at the next sale, the company is sold for a 4x MOIC, that 30 cents becomes $1.20, and the second bite of the apple is actually bigger than the first bite. Remember, as the company grows (which it will, as more businesses are acquired), it will sell for a larger multiple. As

I mentioned previously, my personal record is getting five bites at one company in thirteen years!

Here is a case study in rollover investing from my own career. I once bought a company for $16.4 million. The seller took $12 million home, paid taxes on it, and invested it elsewhere. That allowed him to diversify his assets. The remaining $4.4 million was rolled forward as an investment in my company. Three years later, after I bought seven more companies, I sold the whole business for 13X and got a 4X MOIC. As a result, the original seller got another bite of the apple: a second check for $17.6 million. After that second bite, he had received $29.6 million in total. Let me tell you—that founder now completely understands the power of rollover investing!

TAKE ADVANTAGE OF THE M&A PROCESS

Buy-and-build is a complex process. In fact, I could write an entire book on M&A—and maybe, someday, I will. For now, though, what's important is that you understand the value of this tool to take your business from $100 million or so up to a billion. It is also incredibly valuable if you have a mature company whose organic growth has stalled below 30 percent because buy-and-build could be the key to driving that growth curve back up and keeping it there.

As valuable a tool as it is, there's no question that buy-and-build is both complex and nuanced, especially when private equity is involved. So, let me say it again: I highly recommend that you read *The Private Equity Playbook* and other books about M&A before diving into this world. I also strongly encourage you to consider working with a coach who is experienced in this world (or reaching out to your peer network for more guidance). Now, though, it's time to move on to the next advanced tool you will need to build your empire: strategy and management systems.

KEY TAKEAWAYS

- Mergers and acquisitions (also referred to as M&A, or buy-and-build) are key to boosting a mature company's growth curve above 30 percent and keeping it there.

- Buy-and-build is the art of combining multiple companies together to expand the platform business's geographic reach, build its density, and/or help it pivot.
- For M&A to succeed, you need a fragmented industry, an understanding of what "good" looks like, and a solid strategy.
- You can use the PE pyramid to reap multiple arbitrage.
- M&A has nine main stages: sourcing, outreach, filter, IOI–LOI, diligence, contracts, funding, closing, and integration.
- The best way to convince founders to sell to you is to help them understand the many benefits M&A can bring them.

NINE

Every Empire Needs a
STRATEGY AND MANAGEMENT SYSTEM

A S IMPORTANT AS ALL THE TOOLS WE'VE TALKED about so far are to building your empire—and make no mistake, they are *vitally* important—the tool we're going to discuss in this chapter holds the key to optimizing all of them. It's what will help drive a process of continuous improvement, make you more accountable, and make your results far more predictable. Perhaps most of all, it will help guide you through every stage of growth and make sure you stay on track.

THE EVOLUTION OF STRATEGY

As with so many things in my career, I first learned about strategy and management systems—the tool we're going to focus on in this chapter—from Jack Welch, former CEO of General Electric. During the ten years that I was at GE, Jack taught me (and the world) that business requires strategy, strategy requires initiatives, initiatives require measurement systems, and leadership effectiveness needs to be managed.

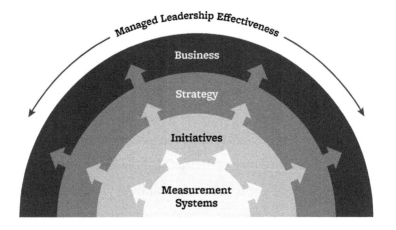

Jack was the first person to create initiatives and measurement systems like this. In fact, he was the first person to create a viable framework by which businesses could keep score and thereby manage their success.

These concepts—let's call them Strategy and Management 1.0—were revolutionary. When GE started implementing them, productivity skyrocketed and results improved dramatically. As I mentioned earlier in the book, in that ten-year period, GE's stock split three times, and GE leaders were coveted worldwide. However, there was a problem. Jack's system supported massive growth, but it didn't lead to consistent results. There was a piece missing; the system was faulty when it came to hiring the right people for the job.

At first, no one understood why GE struggled in this area. When we hired new people, we made sure they had a history of strong results. Despite this, there was only a 50/50 chance they would produce the kinds of results we were looking for. In other words, even though we hired good people who had achieved great results in the past, success was not a foregone conclusion.

Jack's strategy and management system had allowed GE to take off, grow, and outperform all expectations. But the system itself had inherent limitations, and those limitations meant we couldn't consistently achieve our optimal desired outcomes.

CONNECTING TALENT TO VALUE

As great as Jack's strategy was, its limitations were causing problems. *Something* had to be done to fix it—but what? The business world grappled subconsciously with that issue for years until Sandy Ogg—former CHRO at Unilever, operating partner at Blackstone Private Equity, the founder of CEO.*works*, and another great mentor of mine—came along. He found the gap in Jack's system: it put measurement systems in place and emphasized the need to hire good people, but it didn't connect talent to value. (Side note: you can buy Sandy's *Talent to Value* white paper from the CEO.works' website. Believe me, as you work to grow your empire, you will find that investing in this and the other publications he's authored to be money well spent.)

Essentially, Sandy realized that, along with identifying key initiatives that drive value creation, businesses *also* need to consider who in the organization is going to do the work. Then, they need to match the skillsets and the specific situational experience of those people to the actual work being done. For example, suppose you have a B2B business. After reading the last chapter, you know you want to use a combination of organic growth and buy-and-build to go from $100 million to $1 billion. To accomplish this, along with looking for companies to acquire, you decide to hire a new VP of sales. Here's the thing: simply interviewing people who have strong sales backgrounds and great success driving top-line financial results isn't specific enough. To connect talent to value, you should absolutely look for a great salesperson. However, the right candidate will also have experience successfully melding the different sales cultures of multiple companies that were brought together through a buy-and-build in a B2B industry. That's what it means to connect talent to value, and it's what will help ensure you achieve your desired value outcome.

THE CONCEPT OF TABLES

Whether you have 10,000 employees or 10, creating growth initiatives and then finding the right person to own each one is crucial. To see how to do this, let's explore another key part of Sandy's system: the concept of tables.

You may remember that we touched on initiatives in chapter 5. If so, you'll also recall that we discussed identifying the key initiatives that will move the needle forward on your growth. The crucial idea here is that you should focus on *key* initiatives—that means no more than five or six at any one time.

Think about each of your identified key initiatives as conference tables in a conference room. Now, picture who in your organization is going to sit at the tables to talk about, work on, and drive the desired changes. Let's say you have a table (i.e., an initiative) for organic growth, a table for margin improvement, one for M&A, and another one for organic growth on acquired companies. Who sits at each of those tables?

As you think about this, you may realize you already have the right talent in your organization to fill these seats. Or, you may realize there are roles that are critical to driving initiative success that don't yet exist in your company, so you need to add those positions so you can fill them. Furthermore, as you review your tables, you may realize that some of your initiatives should be split into sub-tables. For example, the activity you undertake for price is different from the actions you take to drive volume, so your organic growth table might need to split into a price table and a volume table. Once it does, you will need to ask yourself who is going to make price happen. As you picture who needs to be at that conference table, you might realize you need a VP of sales, a director of pricing, and someone from legal to oversee contract review (to determine which of your contracts have price escalation clauses built-in) and contract language modification (for those contracts that don't have escalation clauses).

At your volume table, on the other hand, you may realize you need to increase your funnel size, find more opportunities, and increase your close rates. For that, you might need a VP of marketing, a VP of sales, and a VP of strategic accounts. If you have different channels, the table might also include your various channel directors. And, of course, *all* of your tables might include an IT person to support the functions of the other people at the table.

IDENTIFY YOUR DRIVERS

When you go through this exercise, you will find there are only a handful of people in your organization who really bend your growth curve and make your key initiatives happen. In my last company, for example, I had about 3,000 employees. After doing this exercise, it was clear that only 22 of them were actually "sitting" at these tables. That's not to say that my other 2,978 employees weren't important. They certainly were—and so are all of *your* other employees.

While the people at the tables are bending the growth curve, your other employees are continuing to service your existing customers and make sure your base business stays on track. However, as vital as they are, they *aren't* super-charging your growth and helping to turn your business into an empire. Connecting talent to value helps you identify who is actually going to bend the growth curve within your organization, so you can hire and retain accordingly.

Since the people at your initiative tables are so important to driving the future growth of your business, it's worth treating them a little differently from everyone else. Once you've identified them (and remember, they may not be your direct reports), empower them to make decisions. If they aren't a VP, give them an executive sponsor from your direct leadership team who can support them in impacting necessary change in your business. It's also important to give them a high degree of access to you. You should also focus on implementing reward structures and supporting their developmental needs (for example, sponsoring their MBAs or sending them to additional training). Bottom line, make it one of your priorities to retain these talented people because they are key to building your empire.

INCREASE YOUR PROBABILITY FOR SUCCESS

I've used the combination of Jack's initiative system and Sandy's talent-to-value system in multiple companies through multiple hold periods and it works perfectly— *every single time.* By implementing this tool, you can confidently and strategically systematize how you bend your business's growth curve, while at the same time maintaining your base business's trajectory. Best of all, by combining these two elements, you can drastically increase your probability of finding success.

Of course, as valuable as this tool is, there are a few things you need to keep in mind in order to maximize its potential. We'll take a look at those things in the next chapter.

KEY TAKEAWAYS

- Implementing a strategy and management system will allow you to optimize all the other tools we've discussed so far.

- Business requires strategy; strategy requires initiatives; initiatives require measurement systems; and leadership effectiveness must be managed.
- Along with identifying key initiatives that drive value creation, you also need to consider who in the organization is going to do the work.
- Hiring the right people requires you to understand how to connect talent to value.
- Think of each of your key initiatives as conference room tables, then identify who needs to sit at those tables to get the job done.
- Once you've identified these key employees, focus on retaining them by treating them differently.

TEN

ACHIEVING MAXIMUM POTENTIAL

N THE LAST CHAPTER, I INTRODUCED YOU TO STRATegy and management systems. Now, I want to refine your understanding of this tool even further. Specifically, I want to share some common pitfalls you should avoid, and then I want to discuss some ways you can increase this tool's efficacy and systematize your outcomes.

COMMON PITFALLS TO AVOID

As you now know, tying strategy to initiatives and connecting talent to value are both incredibly important. However, there are two common mistakes people make when they are putting this type of system into place. First, they have too many people sitting at each of their "tables." Second, they put the wrong people at their tables.

Most of the founders and entrepreneurs I've worked with have a tendency to put the same five or ten people (usually their direct reports) at every single table. That's a mistake. While you can have the same person at multiple tables, more often than not, these five or ten people *aren't the ones doing the work.*

Take your price table, for example. Who is *actually* going to oversee the work of reviewing every single one of your (potentially thousands of) contracts to figure out which have price escalation clauses? It's not going to be your vp of sales! Sure, they may need a seat at your price table, but the person who is overseeing the work (maybe the vp of contract administration or a director of contracts) should also be there.

Similarly, if you put the same people at every table, you'll get yourself into trouble. Take the price table and the volume table, for example. It's entirely appropriate to have your sales leaders at your volume table, but they aren't the right people to put at your price table. If you want to improve margin by improving your purchasing, the coo shouldn't be at that table. Your director of purchasing should, since they are the ones who negotiate contracts with vendors. Remember, you might have an executive sponsor sitting at the table with them to help guide and coach them (and help enforce their decisions), but that sponsor is simply there in a supporting role. As much as possible, the people at your table should be the ones who are actually doing the work (or overseeing it).

USING THE BRIDGE TOOL

Once you've identified your key initiatives and figured out who will make them happen, you are ready to maximize your strategy and management system's potential. That's where this next tool—the bridge—comes in.

The image on the following page shows a basic EBITDA bridge. (Note: you can find this tool, which is simply known as a "bridge," inside Microsoft Excel.) As you can see, we are starting with a base business of $70 million in EBITDA and building out a five-year strategic plan to bend its growth curve up to $259 million in EBITDA.

This bridge incorporates the basic building blocks of growth that we've been talking about throughout this book: organic growth levers, margin improvement, M&A,

and so on. It also accounts for negative things like inflation, as well as the interim plateau that will occur as a result of these positive and negative forces coming together. That's why I love using the bridge tool—it's such a simple and easy way to visualize the basic building blocks of growth. As an empire builder, I highly recommend that you utilize bridges, too. They are incredibly versatile: you can use bridges to build out one-year, three-year, or five-year strategic plans; you can use them to focus on EBITDA, revenue, enterprise value, and more; and you can use them for a business of any size.

5-YEAR STRATEGIC PLAN—EBITDA

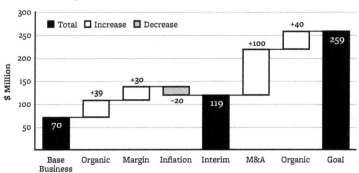

Think about it. You already know you want to grow by 30 percent or better. You know you have levers and tools that will help you do that. Now, you need to put together a road map to get there. That's what the bridge gives you.

When you build a bridge, you need to make some assumptions. For the organic growth block, for example, you may work with your sales team to determine that you can grow your sales volume by 6 percent each year and your price by 3 percent. So, take $70 million (your starting point) and run out five iterations (because it's a five-year plan) of your expected volume and price growth. If you do the math, you'll find that yields an organic growth target of $39 million of EBITDA.

Once you've done this, consider what multiple your business will trade for (you can use the PE pyramid from chapter 4 to help you make this determination). In the bridge above, I assumed a 12x multiple of EBITDA, so adding $39 million of EBITDA for organic growth yields $468 million in shareholder value. When you think of it in those terms, it's easy to see that investing in organic growth is well worth it, because it will add immense value and move your business closer to empire status.

As you begin to use the bridge in your own business, remember: it helps you visualize future growth based on reasonable assumptions. If your assumptions are unrealistic, you'll miss your targets. If your assumptions are too low, you won't push yourself, and your growth will suffer. So, think about what is reasonable for each of the different blocks shown in the chart. And to bring it full circle, consider this: each of these building blocks should become one of the "tables" discussed in the last chapter.

UP YOUR GAME

Now that you have the basics mastered, let's look at how you can use the same bridge to determine enterprise value over a given time period. The following graphic shows the same bridge; this time, our focus is on enterprise value creation. Using a 12X multiple, you are witnessing the same company's progression from an enterprise value of $840 million to $3.1 billion.

As you can see, this tool helps you understand *exactly* how to get to where you want to go, based on the tools we've already covered. And remember, there are so many ways you can use this tool—for revenue, earnings, shareholder value, EBITDA, and more.

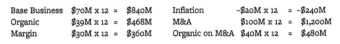

ENTERPRISE VALUE CREATED
by Initiative Using 12x Multiple

(Use the exit multiple you estimate the company will sell for when the work is done
as the multiplier for each initiative. In this example, we use a 12x.)

Base Business	$70M x 12	=	$840M	Inflation	-$20M x 12	=	-$240M
Organic	$39M x 12	=	$468M	M&A	$100M x 12	=	$1,200M
Margin	$30M x 12	=	$360M	Organic on M&A	$40M x 12	=	$480M

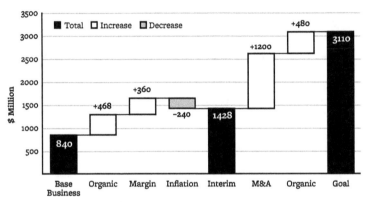

IT WORKS FOR ANY SIZE BUSINESS

You might be thinking to yourself right now, "But Adam, I'm a small business! I don't have $840 million in enterprise value!" No problem: this tool will work for you, too.

It doesn't matter if your business is doing $840 million, $84 million, or $84,000. It doesn't even matter if you have a lemonade stand on the side of the road, and you make $8.40. The tool works regardless of your business's size. To show you what I mean, here's an example of a smaller business. This one is going from $84 million to $311 million (and it would work exactly the same if we scaled it down to an $840 business going to $3,110, or an $84 business going to $311).

ENTERPRISE VALUE CREATED
Scaled Down to Small Business

(Use the exit multiple you estimate the company will sell for when the work is done as the multiplier for each initiative. In this example, we use a 12x.)

Base Business	$7M x 12	=	$84M	Inflation	–$2M x 12	=	–$24M
Organic	$3.9M x 12	=	$46.8M	M&A	$10M x 12	=	$120M
Margin	$3M x 12	=	$36M	Organic on M&A	$4M x 12	=	$48M

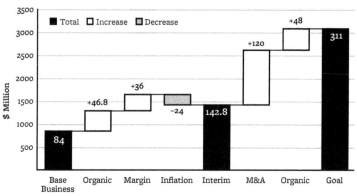

The bridge is the same—all that changes are your numbers. No matter what your starting point is, you can make reasonable assumptions about the concepts we've covered and lay out your road map to massively bend your growth curve and move through the stages of growth.

Throughout your empire-building journey, you're going to be running different-sized businesses at the same time. The bridge will help you visualize and refine your strategy and management systems for all of them, so you can better use the tools we've talked about—organic growth, margin enhancement, strategic pivots, buy-and-build, and so on— to build your empire.

ESTABLISH A REGULAR CADENCE

Once you have your system in place, you will find you can achieve consistent results as you work to create your empire. But it's not enough to simply set the system up and expect it to work flawlessly; you need to systematize the outcome by establishing a cadence of measurement and review. This will allow you to keep score and track not only your company's performance against a particular target but also your people's performance relative to that goal.

Let's go back to our conference room tables for a moment. Each table needs to establish a rhythm that allows the people at it to constantly work toward achieving their assigned initiative. There isn't one right way to do this: maybe they meet weekly, or bi-weekly, or monthly. The important thing is that they have a regular flow that keeps them moving. They have assigned action items and activities that take place regularly. And, they hold themselves accountable to this flow (which should be reviewed and updated annually).

As part of the cadence, it's important that each of your tables establish key performance indicators (KPIS) they can use to make sure they are on target to reach the goals defined in the bridge tool. For example, your volume table might track the number of bids submitted to make sure that number is increasing. They might also track the close rate and monitor the job backlog; these are the types of metrics that will help them understand whether they are on track to hit the defined objectives.

ALWAYS KEEP SCORE

While reviewing metrics is important, it's also helpful to create some kind of scorecard or dashboard where all teams can track their progress. For example, you can create a simple "green, yellow, red" ranking system, where green represents "high performing," yellow corresponds to the "watch list," and red means "action needed." The benefit of creating a scorecard like this is that you can easily assess your risk at any given time. If you're green across the board, you know you're on track to achieve that target for the specified time period. If someone at one of your tables isn't performing well or the metrics aren't coming in at the rate you expect, you might assign a yellow. If someone isn't hitting their targets at all, or if it's an open position that needs to be filled, you can assign a red mark. Anytime you have a yellow, by the way, you will discount your expected target by 25 percent, and anytime you have a red, you will discount by 50 percent. This ranking system gives you a way to predict whether or not you'll achieve your goals; if things aren't looking good, it will also give you time to make adjustments. The problem with most strategic plans that don't incorporate a scorecard approach like this is that everyone makes their plans but never measures anything. Measuring progress like this ensures that everyone stays committed, since what gets measured gets done.

To show you what this might look like, let's say you have a "Margin Improvement" table. You expect $20 million in value from this initiative, and there are three people at the table. The first person is hitting every target. They have a green box next to their name. The second person is hitting only about 70 percent of their targets; they get a yellow box.

The third person is hitting 60 percent of their targets, so they get a yellow box, too. With two yellows and only one green, the overall initiative gets a yellow, which means you are 75 percent on target.

As the leader of the business, when you see a yellow (or a red), you should start meeting with the leaders of the sub-par tables monthly. Talk to them about their initiatives and their KPIs. Hold them accountable to the defined targets, and give them the support they need to get back on track and get the job done.

SYSTEMATIZE YOUR GROWTH

By making sure the right people are at each of your initiative tables, utilizing the bridge tool, and establishing a cadence and measurement system—not to mention implementing all the tools we discussed in the first two sections—you can systematize your growth and turn your business into an empire. And so, in the next (and final) section, we'll look at the final piece of the puzzle: monetizing the empire you've created.

KEY TAKEAWAYS

- When you're populating your conference room tables (i.e., your initiatives), avoid having too many people—or the wrong people—at each table.
- Use the bridge tool to refine and optimize your strategy and management system.
- Establishing a regular cadence and tracking progress toward strategic goals will help ensure that your company and your people stay on track and hit their targets.

SECTION 3 WRAP-UP

Over the course of my career, one lesson has been driven home to me over and over again: success is hard—scaling is harder.

As true as that is, you now have the tools you need to move through the stages of growth and achieve success as an empire builder. You know how to create a solid foundation from which to grow any business in any industry, whether you've started it from scratch, inherited it, or acquired it in some other way. You know how to bend the growth curve by implementing both basic and advanced tools. And, you know how to use your strategy and management system to boost your metrics, consistently hit your targets, and maintain your forward momentum.

At this point, your sophistication is equal to anyone's. No matter what stage of growth your business is currently in, a billion-dollar empire is within your grasp. So now, it's time to talk about the final step on your empire-building journey: monetizing the asset you've worked so hard to create and perfect. I'll meet you there!

MONETIZING YOUR ASSET

We've arrived at the final section. The finish line is in sight. As we embark on the last phase of our empire-building journey, though, I want you to keep one key thing in mind. As I've mentioned throughout the book, part of being a true empire builder is selling the business you've worked so hard to create. And not just once, either—utilize the buy-and-build strategy we discussed in chapter 8 and sell *multiple* times. As I've said before, this has numerous benefits: among other things, it will give you some nice paydays, inject capital into your business so you can grow it more quickly, and increase density and reach so you can penetrate new markets faster.

Why am I telling you this again? Because far too many entrepreneurs, founders, and would-be empire builders think selling their company is a one-and-done deal. If you haven't already done so, *let go of that way of thinking.* Selling your business multiple times is key to diversifying your assets and tapping into the kind of institutional capital you need to rapidly advance through the stages of growth. You can refer back to the PE Pyramid (first introduced in chapter 4 and discussed again in chapter 8) to see the normal inflection points where it might be appropriate to bring in a PE sponsor or other buyer, but the bottom line is that selling your company (whether once or, ideally, multiple times) should be a foregone conclusion in your mind.

That said, selling your business isn't about just hanging out a "For Sale" sign and watching the buyers roll in. To maximize value and attract the kind of buyers you need, you have to package it properly. Remember, the people you want to attract are among the most sophisticated investors and businesspeople on the planet. They're going to be going over every part of your company with a fine-toothed comb, and if it doesn't stand up to their scrutiny, you'll leave money on the table (at best) and lose prospective buyers (at worst). That's why I want to spend this section showing you how to navigate these waters. We're going to kick things off with a discussion about branding, then turn our attention to getting everything in order for a smooth, seamless sale.

A word of caution before we begin: most entrepreneurs I've met think that, because they've built a successful business, they are also experts at *selling* said business. After buying fifty-eight companies from fifty-eight entrepreneurs, I can tell you beyond a shadow of a doubt that assumption is false. Just because you built a great business, it doesn't follow that you know how to sell it. Selling your business is one of—if not *the*—largest financial transaction of your life. Set yourself up for success by utilizing expert help in each step of the process, from working with branding experts (to implement the ideas we'll discuss in chapter 11) to connecting with experts who have successfully sold dozens of businesses (they can help you with the ideas we'll cover in chapters 12 and 13). It would also be wise to read books specifically about exiting successfully—my previous book, *The Exit Strategy Playbook*, is a good place to start.

With all that in mind, it's time to turn our attention toward maximizing the economic potential of your business, so you can turn it into an empire that much faster.

Ready? Me too. Let's do this.

ELEVEN

IT'S TIME TO GET YOUR BRANDING RIGHT

T HROUGHOUT MY CAREER, PEOPLE HAVE ALWAYS said that my greatest superpower is getting buyers to pay way too much for a company. After generating billions of dollars in exits, you know what? I can honestly say it's a good superpower to have.

Here's the thing, though: this superpower doesn't belong to me exclusively. You can develop the same ability—and it starts with understanding that, no matter what industry you're in or whom you're trying to sell to, there is a direct correlation between branding and price.

I recently had a conversation with a CEO I'm coaching about this very topic. To be more specific, we were discussing if (and how) he should rebrand and rename his organization. Rebranding and renaming are things you, as an empire builder, should be thinking about, too. But when is the right time to rebrand? And how can you go about doing so? Let's unpack those questions, and then round out the discussion by talking about how taking a page from Apple's book is the key to maximizing value with your universe of buyers.

THE POWER OF A NAME

Before we dive in, I want to be very clear: if the idea of rebranding is hard for you to swallow, you aren't alone. Lots of founders struggle with the idea. More often than not, though, a brand refresh—usually accompanied by a name change—is exactly what's needed to help a business better connect with its customers.

There are exceptions to this, of course. Take Coca-Cola, for example. In 1985, the company retired its classic formula in favor of "New Coke." It was a rebranding disaster—arguably the worst of all time. People loved Coke. Indeed, they loved it so much that the name of the product had come to represent soda itself! And, as the company found out, making changes to anything as well-known and well-loved as that was a bad idea.

When a brand becomes representative of a product or industry (think Coke, Kleenex, or Q-tips), changing it can do a lot of harm. But for almost everyone else, rebranding is usually a good idea.

THREE SITUATIONS WHERE
REBRANDING MAKES SENSE

You already know that, during my twenty-one-year career as a CEO, I bought fifty-eight companies and built three. What you might not know is that I rebranded *every single one of them*. Granted, rebranding was often difficult for the previous owners to accept. They all really cared about the names of their companies, and they assumed their customers would, too. In every instance, though, they were wrong.

A perfect example of this was a business called Web Service Co. You've heard me talk about Web Service Co before. But would you guess that was the original name of the coin-operated laundry company that I ran from 2003 to 2016? The name certainly doesn't suggest it, and that's my point. William E. Bloomfield and his wife started the company in the 1940s; they tried and tried to come up with a unique name, but every name they liked was taken. Finally, they decided to go with his initials (W.E.B.), and Web Service Co was born. Then, along came the internet. Suddenly, "web" meant something very specific—something that had nothing to do with laundry. When I came in as CEO, I knew it was important to change the name to something more representative of what the company did.

The owners resisted. They thought if they changed the name, sixty years of brand equity would go up in smoke. They worried their customers would leave them—that this would be the laundry equivalent of New Coke. I was insistent, though. I wanted the new name to clearly reflect the services we offered and make sense to prospective customers, so after the founders exited the business and private equity arrived, we changed Web Service Co to WASH Multifamily Laundry Systems.

I believe in being prepared, so (mindful of the founding family's fears) I set up a call center and developed scripts to guide our reps in talking to customers about the rebrand. We were ready for the hordes of angry people who would lash out against us for changing the name. In the end, though, do you know how many people called to complain? Or even to discuss the name change? *Zero.* Nobody cared.

This illustrates an important lesson: *you* may have a sentimental attachment to your brand, but your customers don't. And especially when your company name detracts from your value and confuses people (like a laundry company called Web Service Co), it's time to switch things up.

Detraction and confusion are not the only reasons to consider a refresh, though. If your company's reputation has become tarnished and some portion of your potential customer base sees your organization in a negative light, a name change may be in order. In instances like this, your company has what I refer to as a "damaged brand." It's not that the name itself is misleading or confusing, but it *is* damaged goods. By renaming the company, you can reintroduce your organization and, in doing so, start to change people's perceptions of it.

After coaching so many entrepreneurs, I know what the majority of you reading this are probably thinking right now: "My company's name describes what we do, and my brand isn't damaged. I guess I don't need to rebrand!" Not so fast. Even if your name is clear and your reputation is good, a rebrand may still be in order. This is especially true if your sales are lagging or you aren't hitting your numbers. In those instances, reimagining who you are and then sharing your new and improved brand with the world may be the kickstart your company needs to bring in new customers *and* attract buyers.

MAKE YOUR NAME SIZZLE

The moral of the story is simple: don't fall into the trap of becoming overly attached to your name or your brand. Be willing to pivot, refresh, and shake things up. For optimal results, don't wait until your brand is floundering, either. Rebranding periodically will keep your organization fresh and relevant, and it will ensure your business is attractive to both customers (existing and prospective) and buyers.

When you do refresh, be intentional about it. Put in the time and effort necessary to ensure your new name and brand will appeal to all of your stakeholders. Appeal is important, so don't leave it to chance. Reach out to peer groups or hire a coach to help you objectively decide if you need a refresh. Then, work with a professional marketing firm that specializes in branding to think through exactly what your brand needs to create the kind of impact you want. Remember, you might be an expert at building your business, but that doesn't mean you're an expert in branding it.

I don't want to belabor the point, but I can't overstate how important rebranding is. Far too often, people start a company and give it a name that doesn't maximize that business's economic potential. Sometimes they use their own name. Sometimes they give it a name that sounds charming to them or is synonymous with their core product or service. That may be fine to start, but as you grow and build your empire—and begin adding ancillary revenue streams, expanding into new markets, and/or pivoting—your goal should be to present a more professional and unified face to the market. Your name and your brand should convey who you are and what you do—and it should have some sizzle.

Master that (or work with an expert who has), and—I promise—you will be that much closer to selling your business for maximum value and reaping the full economic potential of the empire you're building.

THE CACHET OF THE APPLE BOX

When you're packaging your business to sell, it's not enough to have a name that sizzles. You also need a brand presence that sizzles. After all, at the end of the day, it's not a computer buying your company—it's a person buying your company. When people are attracted to your brand, they will pay more for it, both because *they* like it and because they know *customers* will like it, too.

Let me illustrate what I mean by talking about the cachet of the Apple box.

For the past decade, I've been conducting a spot poll. It doesn't matter whether I'm giving a guest lecture at a prestigious university to a room full of EMBA candidates or teaching a seminar to entrepreneurs, Fortune 500 executives, and industry leaders—I never skip this poll. First, I ask my attendees to raise their hands if they own at least one Apple device. Every time, 90 percent of them put their hands up. Imagine: these are the best and brightest business minds in the world...and *nine out of ten of them own an Apple device.*

Then, I ask a second question: how many of the people who own an Apple product still have the box their device came in? Once again, 90 percent raise their hands.

This tells me two things. Perhaps most obviously, it tells me Apple has the lion's share of its market. But it's also a clear demonstration that Apple has developed such a brand affinity among its base that its customers cannot bring themselves to throw out the boxes their devices come in. Instead, they stack the empty boxes in their closets or desk drawers and leave them there. It's remarkable when you think about it. The boxes serve no further purpose, and yet, 90 percent of people don't throw them away. What's just as remarkable is that this phenomenon holds another key to building an empire.

IT'S NOT ABOUT BEING BETTER

To understand this, first consider this key point: my informal poll consistently reveals that the 10 percent of people who don't own an Apple device are engineers or tech people. They buy Android-based products because the technology is (arguably) better.

Here's where it gets interesting. Winning the game clearly isn't about being better, at least not exclusively. Apple may not have the best technology, but they have such a large and loyal customer base that they dominate the market anyway. Even though they aren't the best, they have the highest engagement, and that makes all the difference.

Their superiority is demonstrated in other ways, too. For example, remember when we talked about the Oracle of Omaha's suggestion to invest in what you know? If so, you may also remember that, to test his advice, I invested in five specific companies—and Apple was one of them. Well, guess what? In my entire personal portfolio of stocks and investments, the single highest return (more than 600 percent) on any stock I've owned is Apple.

There's a direct correlation between the products they produce, the way they package them, and the financial results they derive. And that leads directly to the moral of *this* story: if you want to grow your business successfully and sell it for the highest price possible, the most important thing you can do is build a culture patterned after the concept of Apple and represented by the Apple box.

BUILD A PEOPLE-FIRST CULTURE

Think back to the second chapter, when we talked about managing for culture, not revenue. Now, consider this: Apple has mastered this foundational advice. Managing for revenue would be like Apple focusing on building the best technology—and that's not the secret to their success. Instead, building a company that people are devoted to is their absolute priority. The fact that customers won't throw their empty boxes away is a testament to how well they've succeeded.

Apple is a people-first organization. They have a strong culture, and their brand reflects that. They've figured out how to take care of their people; in turn, their people take care of their customers, who take care of their revenue and their growth—again, concepts I discussed in chapter 2. On top of that, Apple is transparent about its culture. They've built an entire brand around it, in fact, and people resonate with that brand so much that the vast majority of their customers literally keep the boxes their products came in, despite the fact that those boxes are, for all intents and purposes, useless.

THE "APPLE-EFFECT" IN ACTION

If you can apply the magic of Apple to your own company, you can replicate the affinity it enjoys among its customer base (this is what I refer to as the "Apple-effect"). When you do, you will be able to rise to the top of your field, just as Apple has risen to the top of theirs. And you know what? Buyers will know if you've mastered the Apple-effect, and they will pay far more for your business than they otherwise would.

After reading chapter 2, you already manage for culture. Now, go a step further. Create a brand that reflects the amazing magnet company you've built. You might start by taking a close look at your headquarters. If a buyer came to visit, would they be blown away by how well your HQ communicates your brand? Does your HQ clearly communicate who you are, what you do, and what your core values are? If not, it should; those things are what will give you the home court advantage with your universe of buyers and drive your business's price up.

Get this stuff right, and suddenly, instead of your prospective buyers simply focusing on your EBITDA and the typical multiple your company would trade for, they'll be adding another multiplier. Specifically, they'll be considering how much of a premium they have to pay to own the amazing asset you've built and nurtured.

It's no exaggeration to say that prominently displaying their culture and making sure their names were on point were two of the keys to getting above-market prices for every empire I sold. These things were so important, in fact, that I would make a multi-million dollar investment to get them right. Sometimes, that included building an HQ environment that really spoke to culture and what we had created. Sometimes, it meant updating vehicle wraps, office spaces, and uniforms. I worked with branding consultants to figure out exactly what the brand needed, and then I invested whatever was necessary to make it happen.

If your eyebrows went up reading that I happily spent several million dollars on brand refreshes, then reading about the return on investment will make them go up even more. The ROI for WASH Multifamily Laundry Systems and CoolSys (the refrigeration company I first mentioned in chapter 6) was an additional 1x multiple each—and that kind of return is far from unique. To put that into perspective, if a company had $100 million of EBITDA, and the buyer was willing to pay another 1x because they were enthralled by its culture, brand, and imagery, that would provide an extra $100 million return. The Apple-effect is *that* powerful, and it's something you can and should capitalize on.

BRAND TO ATTRACT CUSTOMERS AND BUYERS

Ultimately, as you're building your empire, it's not enough to just focus on taking care of your customers. You also have to think about how well you are setting yourself up to attract buyers, and branding plays a significant role in doing just that.

Now that you understand the importance of branding to successfully sell your company, it's time to spend some time thinking about your exit path. In the next chapter, we'll discuss the right time to sell, then dive into the basic universe of buyers.

KEY TAKEAWAYS

- As you build your empire, periodically take time to think about rebranding and renaming.
- Your name should clearly communicate who you are and what you do—and it should have a little bit of sizzle, too.
- Working with consultants is a great way to make sure your name and your brand maximize the economic potential of your business.

- Master the "Apple-effect" to drive your business's value up among your universe of buyers.
- Don't overlook the importance of investing in your brand. In terms of ROI, it may be the single most important thing you do.

---- TWELVE ----

CHOOSING
AN EXIT PATH

N THE LAST CHAPTER, WE TALKED ABOUT HOW IMPORT-
ant branding is to attract both the right customers *and*
the right buyers. Branding is about playing the long game;
while it's absolutely one of the foundational pieces for maximizing the value of your asset, it's not something you can
slap into place in a desperate attempt to attract good buyers fast. Ideally, branding is something you get right years
before you're ready to sell. So, now that you know how to
do that, let's assemble the rest of what you need to know
about exiting successfully.

A quick reminder: as you go through the information
in this chapter (and chapter 13), keep in mind that selling

your business doesn't necessarily mean riding off into the sunset, never to be seen again. It *can* mean that, if that's what you want, but in the context of empire building, it's far more likely to mean bringing in a partner with the capital and expertise necessary to get your business to the next stage of growth. That said, whether your goal for exiting is to move on from your business completely or stay on and grow it, your priority as an empire builder should be to sell smart *and* for maximum value.

FINDING THE RIGHT TIME TO SELL

Before we launch into our discussion of what you need to do to prepare for a successful exit, I want to address a question that I'm sure is on your mind. That question is, of course, *when is the right time to sell?*

The answer to that has two parts. First part: take a look back at the PE Pyramid (covered in chapters 4 and 8). Each of the rungs in the pyramid reveals natural inflection points where it makes sense to sell. For example, there's a natural sell point around $50 million in EBITDA. Why? Because at that point, you can bring in a new PE sponsor to help you grow to $100 million. Then, at $100 million in

EBITDA—another natural sell point—you can bring in a new PE firm that can help you grow to $200 million in EBITDA.

Before we go on, I do want to note that it's typically at these various sell points where multiple expansion occurs. However, with so many PE firms looking for companies to buy in recent years, these sell points have been flexing down a bit. In other words, buyers in any given rung of the pyramid that have capital to deploy are reaching down to find good companies a little lower on the PE pyramid in order to put their money to work. So, treat the PE pyramid as a general guideline about when to sell, rather than as a hard-and-fast rule.

As useful as they are, the inflection points of the PE Pyramid are just one part of the answer to when you should sell. The second part of the "right time to sell" equation comes down to what I refer to as the *Rule of 130*. Take your age, then add the percentage of your net worth that's tied up in your business to that number. If the sum is 130 or greater, it's time to think about exiting your business (either wholly or partially).

I created the Rule of 130 to help entrepreneurs and founders mitigate risk. When you own a business, it's a non-liquid investment. The money you have tied up in it isn't money you can spend; it's not cash in the bank. The Rule of 130 helps you determine when your personal risk is too high.

Many of the entrepreneurs I speak with assume that, if their sales are strong, there's no risk to their existing business, but the last few years have shown us just how inaccurate that is. If your number is over 130, you should be thinking about asset diversification. You should be worried about the impacts of a bad economy, a global pandemic, or a war—all of which are things we've experienced over the last few years. Any of these events could drastically alter the trajectory of your business or destroy it completely; as a result, your net worth could be wiped out, and if your number is over 130, it's likely you wouldn't have time to recover from that before retirement. The Rule of 130 is key to identifying your individual risk equation and determining if it's time to sell.

YOUR PROSPECTIVE UNIVERSE OF BUYERS

Now that you understand *when* to sell, the next logical question is, *whom do I sell to?* To answer that, let's talk about the universe of buyers.

You may remember from earlier in the book that PE buys about 50 percent of the companies on the planet. However, PE is far from the only type of buyer out there. Your ideal buyer will vary depending on your goals and objectives, so let's go through them one by one.

A note before we get started: there are many nuances to choosing the right buyer for your business that are beyond the scope of this book. However, I have no intention of leaving you hanging. My last book, *The Exit Strategy Playbook*, discusses the universe of buyers in far more detail than we can do here, so read it carefully when you start preparing to exit.

Strategic Buyers

The first type of buyer I want to discuss is what's known as a *strategic buyer*. Simply put, a strategic buyer is a company that buys another company. Morgan Stanley was a strategic buyer of E*Trade. Facebook was a strategic buyer of WhatsApp. Amazon was a strategic buyer of Whole Foods. Importantly, while these are all examples of large companies acquiring other large companies, the size of the company or how it's structured doesn't matter.

Businesses become strategic buyers for a variety of reasons. They may seek to expand into new geography. They may want to build density in existing markets. Maybe they want to add capability, like a new technology or tool, or access a new customer vertical. Heck, in chapter 8, we discussed how you can become a strategic buyer to accelerate your company's growth. Bottom line, a strategic buyer is executing on a strategy, and they believe the business they're acquiring will help them accelerate that strategy.

There are two types of strategic buyers: ones that keep the lights on and ones that are going to turn the lights off. If you sell to a strategic buyer that plans to keep the lights on, they generally want you to stay on with the company. No, you won't be a majority shareholder, but as we've talked about multiple times, that's okay. You'll get the capital you need to accelerate growth, and you may be able to become a rollover investor and continue your own personal wealth story while you continue to scale your company.

If you're selling to a strategic buyer that wants to turn the lights off, things look very different. These kinds of buyers are not interested in your ongoing involvement in the company. They're buying your customers, your technology, and your worker bees. They're going to harness all the synergies between your company and theirs, and then they're going to ask you to exit stage left.

CASE STUDY: HARTLAND INSURANCE

To help you understand what it can look like to sell to a strategic buyer that wants to keep the lights on, I want to share a case study with you. You may recall from chapter 1 that my brother and I owned an insurance agency called Hartland Insurance. It had $4.2 million in revenue and $1.7 million in EBITDA.

The Rule of 130 dictated that my brother needed to sell. He was sixty-three, and about 90 percent of his net worth was tied up in the company. However, he wanted to keep working at the company. He wanted to become a rollover investor, too. Because Hartland had a stagnant growth profile and was too small for a financial buyer (we'll talk about them next) to turn into a platform company, we decided to look for a strategic buyer that planned to keep the lights on.

We found one (we'll talk more about how to do that in chapter 13) and sold them the business. Several years later, my brother is still happily working at Hartland Insurance. He's also a rollover investor, and in the next year or two, when the new owners take the company public, not only will he have the satisfaction of knowing he helped build an empire, but he'll also get a second substantial bite of the apple.

Financial Buyers

Next up: financial buyers. Generally speaking, these are the buyers I personally like to target when I'm looking to build an empire. Financial buyers are primarily private equity firms. You may recall from our discussions about them in chapters 4 and 8 that they supply the capital you need to supercharge your growth. You are still responsible for delivering on strategy, operations, and the day-to-day running of the business. Unlike with a strategic buyer, where there's a chance that you may not get multiple bites of the apple, with a financial buyer, you certainly will.

Alternative Buyers

As an empire builder, it makes the most sense to focus on either strategic buyers or financial buyers. Of course, there are other types of buyers: owner-operators, MLBOS (management-led buyouts), ESOPS (employee stock ownership plans), SPACS (special purpose acquisition companies), and even IPOS (initial public offerings). However, in the context of what you're trying to do, these buyers are generally not ideal for helping you achieve your empire-building dreams.

BUILD TO SELL

I see it all the time: a founder wakes up and thinks to themselves, "I'm pushing sixty-five. I better sell my business, and I better do it *fast*." They put no thought or preparation into it—and the end result is a less-than-desirable outcome. To get the kind of outcome you want, don't make this mistake. Make sure you understand what type of buyer is ideal for your needs. Most of all, create a plan that will allow you to sell smart and for maximum value.

Educate yourself about when you should sell so you can start preparing well in advance. Hopefully, you've been building to sell from day one, but if not, plan on spending about three years getting ready to exit. Yes, it can be done more swiftly—I routinely help people get their business ready to sell in just six months—but that's not ideal.

There's a lot of prep work (which we'll cover in the final chapter) needed to exit successfully; giving yourself time to get it all done—and done well—is key to achieving the kind of outcome you want.

KEY TAKEAWAYS

- Selling smart should be a key part of your empire-building strategy.
- Finding the right time (or times) to sell comes down to two things: whether your business is at a natural "sell" point and what your personal risk is (according to the rule of 130).
- There are several types of buyers that can help you build your empire. Which one you choose depends on your specific goals, objectives, and situation.
- Building an empire means building your business in order to eventually sell it—ideally, not once, but multiple times.

THIRTEEN

The Final Step: PREPARING TO SELL

WHEN YOU APPLY THE INFORMATION IN THIS book to your business, you'll build an organization that can thrive and scale in any economic environment. You'll get a business that does right by its customers and its people. And, you'll get a business that is eminently sellable—for maximum value—to the universe of buyers we talked about in the last chapter.

To bring the sale home, though, you need to get your house in order. Not only that—you also need to bring in some key players to maximize your outcome. Ready for the final pieces to the empire-building puzzle? Then roll up your sleeves, and let's get to work.

GET YOUR HOUSE IN ORDER

Whether this is your first sale or your second (or your third, fourth, or even fifth), getting maximum value requires a lot of prep work. Buyers expect your house to be in order, and if it isn't, you'll leave money on the table. What do I mean by "get your house in order"? Simple: get the financial reporting of the business right. Separate any real estate you own. Make sure you have a solid growth story. And, make sure *you're* ready for the level of scrutiny that's going to come your way. Given how important each of these things is, let's go over each of them in more detail.

#1: Fix Your Financial Reporting

If you're like every other entrepreneur or business owner on the planet, your normal goal is to minimize taxes and keep as much of your net income as humanly possible. To accomplish that goal, you probably write off everything you can against your business: the private jet you fly for your family's benefit but also use for occasional business trips.

The boat you own to go fishing that you occasionally take clients out on. The $100,000/year you pay your spouse to work in the business a few hours each month. These are all proper tax write-offs, right (*wink wink*)? The list of creative ways entrepreneurs minimize tax liability goes on and on because we are hardwired to find ways to add lifestyle expenses into our business that decrease our taxable income. When you're selling a business, though, things suddenly change.

Buyers will ask you for three years of financial statements so they can determine your business's revenue and EBITDA trajectory over time and come up with an offer based on those. Be prepared by making sure those statements maximize the true EBITDA. Let me be clear, this does not mean you stop paying your spouse or never fly on a private jet again. It doesn't mean you sell the boat, either. What it does mean is that you get qualified and experienced accountants to review your financial reports using generally accepted accounting practices (GAAP), identify those lifestyle expenses, and add them back in as appropriate adjustments to EBITDA. These specific expenses won't go forward under new ownership, and you'll want to get credit for them when selling.

It's not just about how you report financials and what expenses are included. You also need to think about how you operate your business while you own it to maximize EBITDA well in advance of a sale. For example, let's say that you need an expensive piece of equipment. If you lease rather than buy, the lease hits your operating expenses. That's a negative to your EBITDA, which means it will lower the price you get paid for the company. However, if you buy the asset, it's considered a capital expenditure. Capital expenditures fall below the EBITDA line, which means that your earnings will be higher, and you can get a higher price when you sell.

Making sure you have the right expense structures isn't something you should try to do on your own. You need the help of an outside accounting firm that can help you prepare your financials in advance of the sale to maximize EBITDA.

Accountants can also do a sell-side quality of earnings (Q of E) report. Remember how I said the buyer will ask you for three years' worth of financials? Well, the very next thing they'll do is hire someone to do a Q of E on your business. The buyer's aim is to make sure everything in the Q of E goes their way because that will lower how much they have to pay for your company. As a seller and an empire builder, don't leave this up to chance. Being able to hand your buyer a sell-side Q of E along with your adjusted financial statements will show them exactly what your true EBITDA is and demonstrate that you're a savvy seller who understands how to play the game.

#2: Separate Your Real Estate

As you've been taking your business through the stages of growth, there's a good chance that you've collected some real estate. I'm going to level with you, though—no buyer wants it (unless real estate is the business you're selling). That means you need to separate your real estate from the rest of your business and put fair market leases in place. Doing so will pay dividends later, as well, because when you sell the company, you can keep your real estate, collect income from it, and eventually sell it, too.

Listen, to get the highest valuation possible, you have to make it your number one priority to do everything you can to make the universe of buyers like your business. Keeping real estate wrapped up in what you've built doesn't support this goal; it just makes things harder. So be smart; get rid of the real estate barrier before you list your company for sale.

#3: Tell Your Growth Story

If you've implemented all the advice I've shared through-out the book, you're running a really strong company. Your numbers are good, and you have a great growth tra-jectory. Now, it's time to tell buyers your growth story. Share what levers you're pulling. Talk about the M&A strategies you've implemented that have allowed you to bend the growth curve to 30 percent or more. Describe the strategy and management systems you've put into place to maximize the potential of operating the business. Make sure they understand what processes and technol-ogy you're using to enhance your margins. Show them the amazing culture you've built, and give them a chance to see you have great people who can maintain the growth curve with or without you.

To start crafting your growth story, it may be helpful to think through the following questions:

- **What type of succession planning and team development do you have in place?** Buyers want to know the business can survive and thrive even if you aren't there.

- **What is your organic (and inorganic) growth trajectory?** This includes the levers of growth that we talked about in chapter 6.

- **Are there merger and acquisition opportunities?** Remember, buy-and-build is a key tool for bending the growth curve, so making sure buyers know there are other companies out there that could supplement yours can make your business even more valuable.

- **Can your business scale efficiently?** Financial buyers in particular want to build a platform that can grow quickly. Show them your business has simple, repeatable processes *and* utilizes technology effectively. If your business has bottlenecks, develop a plan to address them so your buyer won't have to.

- **How does your business perform during tough economic times?** The economy is cyclical. It's not a question of *if* we'll encounter a recession or other difficulties in the economic climate, but *when*. Buyers will pay far more for a business that can weather down cycles and continue to thrive.

You can't depend on buyers to see this story for themselves; you need to craft it for them. As you do, make sure your growth story aligns with your historical performance and that it's forward-looking enough to be exciting.

#4: Be Ready for Scrutiny

This last point may be short, but that doesn't make it any less important. Every time you go through a sale process, *you* are on display. Every single thing you do and say will affect what your buyer thinks of you and how much they are willing to pay for your company. Yes, industry multiples and competition are important, but they give buyers a range for determining their offer. Your behavior, demeanor, and conduct will rack up intangible points or give them away, and those points will absolutely impact where in the range their offer falls.

MAXIMIZE YOUR OUTCOME BY BRINGING IN THE RIGHT PEOPLE

As you can see, prep work is important. However, it's just one part of selling smart. Remember in the introduction to this section when I cautioned you against thinking that just because you're an expert at building and running your business, you'll also be an expert at selling it? I want to reissue that warning again here: unless you've sold businesses dozens of times, you are *not* an expert. That's why the other piece of exiting successfully is bringing in the right people to help you achieve the kind of outcomes you want.

There are plenty of sharks out there who will happily take your company off your hands for less than it's worth. To protect yourself and ensure you get every penny you deserve, you need to surround yourself with good people. Specifically, you need a competent accountant, a savvy tax advisor, an experienced specialty lawyer, and a good investment banker (or broker, if you're a small business). Let's talk about each of them—and where to find them—in turn.

#1: Accountants

We talked earlier about the importance of getting a good accountant to help you get your financial statements in order and do a sell-side Q of E. But your accountant will do so much more than that.

Think back to chapter 8, when we talked about the stages of M&A. One of the most intense of those stages is diligence. I've said it before, and I'll say it again: for the seller, diligence can feel like a proctology exam that never ends. Having a top-notch accountant on your team will help you get through it with flying colors. They will normalize your accounting practices, make sure your EBITDA is correct (and as high as possible), and help you navigate both the preparation and the actual sale process.

Your business's size will dictate where you look for your accountant. If your revenue is under $10 million, look for a small local or regional firm. If your revenue falls between $10 million and $50 million, you'll want to use a small regional or multiregional firm. If your revenue is $50 million–$250 million, hire a multiregional or tier-two national firm. And, if your revenue is above $250 million, bring in a tier-two national firm or a Big 4 firm.

#2: Tax Advisors

Selling your business—whether it's your first time or your fifth—is one of the biggest financial transactions of your life. To retain as much of that payday as possible, you need an experienced tax advisor.

Tax advisors can help you understand how best to prepare for the windfall that's coming. For example, many entrepreneurs who live in states with high income tax rates try to move to protect their money. A good tax advisor can help you understand how to do this correctly (hint: never move the year of the sale) so that you establish residency appropriately in the new state. This is just one example of how a tax advisor can help you; there are so many more. Ultimately, a competent advisor will equip you with solid strategies to keep as much money in the bank as possible.

The same advice about finding an accountant holds for tax advisors. In fact, in many instances, the firm you partner with for accounting help will also have tax advisors. That makes things easier—while your accountant and your tax advisor will almost always be two different people, you can leverage one firm for both experts.

#3: Legal Counsel

Selling your business for maximum value requires legal help. My advice: work with a lawyer who specializes in selling businesses. If you don't, the risks are all too real. I see entrepreneurs get less-than-desirable contract terms all the time when they use a generalist rather than a specialist in this area. There are attorneys out there who do nothing but buy and sell companies all day long. Those are the folks you want to have on your side.

In my experience buying and selling companies, I have found that specialists often charge a higher hourly rate than the generalists who spend their time on minor, run-of-the-mill issues. However, because these specialists are experts, they know exactly what points to argue and understand exactly what terms to focus on. In other words, competent counsel leads to a fast deal, which can save money overall. And, using a specialist can decrease your risks and trailing liabilities post-close. I can't emphasize this point enough: when you're selling your business, work with a lawyer who specializes in this area of practice. It will save you time, money, and a lot of unnecessary headaches.

To select a firm, I recommend using the Internet Legal Research Group (ILRG). Specifically, type "top 350 law firms public legal" into your internet search browser; their latest rankings of the top 350 law firms in the US (arranged by number of attorneys) will appear. From there, narrow the list down by size. For example, if your revenue falls below $10 million, you'll want to focus on local small or regional firms on the list. If your revenue is between $10 million and $50 million, look for small regional or multi-regional firms on the list. If your revenue is between $50 million and $250 million, look for the multiregional and tier-two national firms included on the list. And, if your revenue is above $250 million, you'll want to reach out to the tier-two national or top-tier firms on the list.

#4: Investment Banker/Broker

Finally, you're going to need an investment banker or broker. (A quick note before we go on: investment bankers come in different sizes and work with medium to large businesses. If you have a small business, you will most likely work with a broker, not an investment banker, but they fulfill the same function.) These are the experts who will guide you through the long and arduous sales process we talked about in chapter 8. They prepare the marketing materials required, send them out to the right prospective buyers, help you achieve maximum value, *and* help you reach your goals. Want to stay involved in your business, like my brother in our insurance agency? An investment banker or broker will help you find a financial buyer or a strategic buyer who will keep the lights on. Want to sail off into the sunset? Your investment banker or broker will help bring in strategic buyers who want to turn the lights off. Whatever results you're looking for, your investment banker or broker will help you get them.

To really get a sense of their value, think about this. All sale processes follow a tried-and-true template that savvy buyers are familiar with. As a rookie seller, you may not be. Your investment banker or broker will help you get through it with flying colors. First, they'll draft what's known as a "one-page teaser." This is simply a document that describes the company being offered for sale on a no-name basis and in a very generic way. They'll send it out to a number of potential buyers (generally around one hundred or so). If a potential buyer is interested, they'll have them sign an NDA in order to learn more. Let's say that thirty prospective buyers sign the NDA; the investment banker or broker will help you whittle that list down to the ten most promising. Those folks will get what's called a "fireside chat," which is an opportunity for you to sit down (virtually) with them for an hour and tell your company's story (and yes, your investment banker or broker will coach you through how to handle the fireside chat).

After the fireside chat, they'll send all thirty of the prospective buyers a CIP (confidential information presentation) or CIM (confidential information memorandum). These are essentially prospectuses that go into more detail about your company: its history, who the leadership team is, what it does, what customers it serves, and so on.

Once the buyers have had a chance to review the prospectus, the investment banker or broker will ask them to send in an indication of interest (IOI). The top five to ten who do (depending on bid separation) will get management meetings. These are four-hour meetings that usually include a dinner or some type of social interaction. After the meetings are over, the investment banker or broker will start asking for refresh bids or letters of intent (LOIs). And throughout this entire process, they'll also be keeping the competitive tension high so you can get the best price possible.

Hopefully, you can see that there's just no way to get maximum value for your company without a good investment banker or broker at your side—coaching you, negotiating for you, and marketing your company.

Just like with accountants, tax advisors, and lawyers, your company's size dictates the size of the investment banking firm you'll work with. Under $4 million of EBITDA? Look for a small local boutique firm. Between $4 million and $10 million of EBITDA? Go with a small local or regional firm. If your EBITDA falls between $10 million and $50 million, look for a regional or tier-two national firm. If you have $50 million to $100 million of EBITDA, go with a tier-two national firm or a top-tier firm. If your EBITDA exceeds $100 million, the largest investment banks are the way to go.

MIND YOUR PS & QS

Be really careful how you conduct yourself during the social part of each management meeting. I've seen sellers drink far too much and spill information that hurt them. For example, let's say you've had a few martinis and a buyer walks up to you and says, "I bet you're really tired of doing these management meetings. I used to do them a lot when I was a CEO. I know how grueling they can be." Those drinks have loosened your tongue, and you respond, "I'm actually doing okay. There's only a few of them on the schedule." It seems innocent enough, but what you've just done is tell the buyer that you don't have a lot of interested parties, and they may be able to come in with a lower number than they originally planned.

Remember, you're swimming with sharks. They're going to do what they can to get information from you. Your job is to keep your head so you don't give anything away.

I've also seen deals sink when people drink too much and then try to drive themselves home. Trust me: no buyer wants to take on the kind of risk that comes along with a potential DWI charge, especially if the seller is planning to stay on in any capacity. So, mind your Ps & Qs. Your investment banker or broker will coach you on how to act during these meetings. Pay attention to what they have to say, and at the same time, remember to use common sense.

TIME WELL SPENT

The typical sales process takes about four to six months. Granted, I've sold companies for over half a billion dollars in just three weeks. Those sales included all of these steps, just on a greatly condensed timeline. But normally, plan to spend about six months on this, and plan to hire the right people to help you every step of the way. That's key to selling smart, and it's key to becoming a true empire builder.

KEY TAKEAWAYS

- Selling your business for maximum value requires a lot of preparation. You need to get your financial statements in order, separate your real estate, and develop a compelling growth story.
- Maximize your outcome by bringing in a competent accountant, tax advisor, attorney, and investment banker (or broker).
- Be careful how you conduct yourself during social engagements with buyers. You don't want to sour the deal or give away key information by drinking too much and making a foolish mistake.

SECTION 4 WRAP-UP

Congratulations—you've done it. You've made it to the end of our journey together. You now have all the tools you need to turn your business into a billion-dollar empire.

Of course, not everybody who reads this book is focused on reaching a billion dollars. And that's okay. Whatever your ultimate goal is—whether it's to create a billion-dollar business, take your company to seven figures (and keep it there), or create a sustainable life-style enterprise—you now have what you need to build a strong business *and take it as far as you want to go.*

When we set out on our journey together, I promised you this would be a book of action. And it is. I've given you the tools you need to take to create the foundation for your empire. I've given you the foundation you need to build what you know and create a best-in-class company that attracts and retains top talent. I've shown you how to get your unit-level economics right so you can build your startup into the perfect million-dollar business. I've told you how to leverage private equity to supercharge your growth. I've given you the keys to pulling the right organic growth levers and enhancing margin so you can bend your growth curve upward of 30 percent and keep it there. And I've let you in on the secrets of buy-and-build, strategy and management systems, and monetizing your asset.

Ultimately, the steps I've shared with you throughout the book are the same steps I've used to build not one, not two, but *three* different empires—in just twenty-one years. They're the steps that have helped me personally create billions of dollars in exits for my shareholders. And, if you apply them, they are the steps that will help you do the same.

You have all the practical tools and knowledge you need to embark on your journey. You're ready. All that's left now, my fellow empire builder, is to go out and do it. I'll be rooting for you.

ACKNOWLEDGMENTS

It takes a village to produce a great book, and *Empire Builder* is no exception. I have the deepest gratitude to my entire village, each of whom has been instrumental in helping me bring Empire Builder to life.

First, I would like to express my heartfelt gratitude to Kristin Clark, my invaluable writing coach, with whom I have collaborated on numerous endeavors. Without Kristin's exceptional skill and expertise, the creation of *Empire Builder* would have resulted in a disordered amalgamation of literary chaos. Her contribution has been instrumental in shaping this book into its polished form. You can find Kristin online at *elitecontentcreation.net*.

My deepest thanks to Nicole Jobe (*coppermountainbooks .com*), who provided skilled and thorough developmental and line editing; Ami Hendrickson (*amihendrickson.com*), who helped me craft the book description; John van der Woude (*jvdwdesigns.com*), who designed the cover and interior graphics and assisted with layout; and Laura Cail (*linkedin.com/in/transformationsbylauracail*), whose proofreading helped ensure that the book you are reading is of the highest quality.

My sincere thanks also to Ron Butler (*ronniebutler.com*), who has narrated each of my books with exceptional skill.

And finally, I want to extend my deepest appreciation to Kelly Teemer of Teems PR, LLC for her masterful help with the marketing for this book. You can connect with Kelly at *linkedin.com/in/kellyteemer*.

ABOUT THE AUTHOR

Adam Coffey is a bestselling author who spent twenty-one years as president and CEO building three national empires for nine private equity sponsors. In each case, Adam was at the helm for multiple shareholder groups as the businesses grew, raised capital, and changed hands.

Adam's first company, Masterplan, was a medical device service company owned by Three Cities Research (NYC) and Camden Partners (Baltimore) that was subsequently sold after his departure to Berkshire Partners (Boston) in 2007 and later became a division of Aramark (NYSE: ARMK) in 2011.

His second company, WASH Multifamily Laundry, a commercial laundry service company, started as a family-owned business that was subsequently sold to Code Hennessy & Simmons (Chicago), Twin Bridge Capital Partners

(Chicago), and Thrivent Financial Services (Minneapolis) in 2008, and then again to EQT Partners (Stockholm) in 2015.

Adam's third company, CoolSys, was a commercial refrigeration and HVAC service company owned by the Audax Group (Boston) and that was sold in 2019 to Ares Management (NYSE: ARES).

In 2021, Adam founded CEO Advisory Guru LLC. He serves as a management consultant and independent director to private equity portfolio companies, founders, family offices, and C-suite executives. His areas of specialty include CEO coaching, diligence, M&A, growth strategy, talent to value, exits, and public speaking. His impactful seminars have generated millions in revenue, solidifying his position as one of the world's top speakers.

A former GE executive, alumnus of the UCLA Anderson Executive Program, and veteran of the US Army, Adam is married and has three children. He resides in Westlake, Texas, with his wife and youngest daughter.

Learn more about Adam at his website, *AdamECoffey .com*, or on LinkedIn at *linkedin.com/in/adamecoffey*.

Printed in the USA
CPSIA information can be obtained
at www.ICGtesting.com
LVHW021613081224
798629LV00037B/764

* 9 7 9 8 9 8 9 0 4 9 1 1 0 *